I0277143

DON'T GET ME STARTED

Also by Mitchell Symons

Non-fiction
Forfeit!
The Equation Book of Sports Crosswords
The Equation Book of Movie Crosswords
The You Magazine Book of Journolists (four books, co-author)
Movielists (co-author)
The Sunday Magazine Book of Crosswords
The Hello! Magazine Book of Crosswords (three books)
How To Be Fat: The Chip And Fry Diet (co-author)
The Book of Criminal Records
The Book of Lists
The Book of Celebrity Lists
The Book of Celebrity Sex Lists
The Bill Clinton Joke Book
National Lottery Big Draw 2000 (co-author)
That Book
This Book
The Other Book
The Sudoku Institute (co-author)
Why Girls Can't Throw
Where Do Nudists Keep Their Hankies?
This, That and The Other
My Story (with Penny Symons and Jack Symons)

Fiction
All In
The Lot

Children's books
How to Avoid A Wombat's Bum
Why Eating Bogeys Is Good For You

DON'T GET ME STARTED

MITCHELL SYMONS

BANTAM PRESS

LONDON · NEW YORK · TORONTO · SYDNEY · AUCKLAND

TRANSWORLD PUBLISHERS
61–63 Uxbridge Road, London W5 5SA
A Random House Group Company
www.rbooks.co.uk

First published in Great Britain
in 2007 by Bantam Press
an imprint of Transworld Publishers

A CIP catalogue record for this book
is available from the British Library.

ISBN 9780593059944

Addresses for Random House Group Ltd companies outside the UK
can be found at: www.randomhouse.co.uk
The Random House Group Ltd Reg. No. 954009

The Random House Group Ltd makes every effort to ensure that the
papers used in its books are made from trees that have been legally
sourced from well-managed and credibly certified forests. Our paper
procurement policy can be found at:
www.randomhouse.co.uk/paper.htm

Designed by www.carrstudio.co.uk
Illustrations by Ruth Murray. www.ruthmurray.net
Printed by Clays Ltd, Bungay, Suffolk

2 4 6 8 10 9 7 5 3 1

To Penny, Jack and Charlie

oy-bands. And their managers. Organizatio
like hotels – having 'writers in residenc
ompous or what? In fact, I'm being
ttle hypocritical as I used to be th
riter in Residence at the TravelMot
odge Inn in West Coventry where I w
he man responsible for writing the boo
opy for the restaurant's most popul
arter: Prawn Cocktail. 'Tender, plum
tlantic prawns [...] a bed of cri
eberg lettuce [...] n Marie Ro
uce, [...]ished [...] wist of lemo
nd preserved [...] an
utter.' I [...] memorab
hrase 'We [...] environme
o please he [...] nergy
e-using [...] don[...] like
past ab[...] Go, girl!'[...]
orts progr[...] music as
ackground [...] s o[...]ectacul
ies. The na[...]win[...]m-en[...]redits
alf the w[...]h of [...]een [...] TV ju
hen y[...] ca
st. Ads [...] Col
arrell [...] No he
ot, he's [...] allowing
lly amo[...]rts so th
hey ca[...] target for promp
ess. For [...] flights fr[...] London
ice take nine[...] minutes an[...] ot the tw
ours on the ticket. So even when th
lane takes off twenty minutes late,
n still arrive on time. TV sports presente
escribing something as 'a big ask
eople calling everyone – even the
hildren – 'mate'. Garbled small 'print'

CONTENTS

NOT SO MUCH GRUMPY AS FURIOUS

There's a scene in the 1953 film, *The Wild One*, where Marlon Brando, playing the prototypical Hell's Angel, is asked what he's rebelling against. 'Whaddya got?' he replies.

Well, that's how I feel when I'm asked what it is I'm so damned angry about.

Whaddya got?

And it's not just the usual suspects – politicians, hospital waiting lists, crime etc. – it's also the (supposedly) little things like pop-ups on the internet inviting us to buy software to stop pop-ups, being charged £3.20 for a small bottle of water in a hotel room minibar and fabulously wealthy film actors telling us that their 'first love is the theatre'.

When I'm done venting my spleen or, more likely, merely pausing for breath as my spleneticism knows no bounds, it's my friends' chance to unburden themselves. And they do.

So it's not just me who's spitting blood, it's also my friends and, by all accounts, their friends too. We're angry. Like Peter Finch in the film *Network*, we want to yell: 'I'm as mad as hell and I'm not going to take this any more!'

You'll note, by the way, that I said 'angry' and not 'grumpy'. I know that grumpy is the word of the moment – you might even say that it was all the rage. Except it isn't. There's no rage in grumpiness – just grim acceptance. The fact is, your average grump even enjoys his little whinges, whereas we angries risk cardiac arrest every time we open our mouths. We are, if you like, the provisional wing of the Grumpy Movement: they're the infantry; we're the commandos.

Anger is to grumpiness what a bottle of absinthe is to a half of mild and bitter or an AK47 is to a walking stick held aloft in a bit of a strop.

Let me give you some examples: People complaining about the weather, the use of 'n' instead of 'and', the word 'affix' as in 'Please affix your stamp here' on official letters, 'blonde' TV presenters with bad roots are all annoying and might even make delicate souls feel grumpy. But to arouse genuine boil-in-the-bag anger requires more, much more – like cyclists treating red traffic lights as optional, people who pronounce the 8th letter of the alphabet as 'haitch', tripping over able-bodied beggars in London, and Michael Winner.

Nevertheless, there's no point in going from 0–100 – or Graham Norton to Brian Sewell – without pausing to savour the horrors en route. So, taking a lead from Dante who had nine circles of hell, I've arranged the book so that we move incrementally from the *annoyance* of the

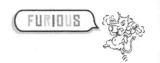

entries in Chapter 1 through to the *aggravation* in Chapter 2, the *exasperation* of Chapter 3, the *irascibility* of Chapter 4, the *outrage* of Chapter 5, the *fury* of Chapter 6 culminating in the *raging fury* of Chapter 7.

But one theme runs through the entire book: from the beginning of Chapter 1 to the end of Chapter 7.

We've had enough.

We're mad as hell and we're not going to take it any more.

DON'T GET ME STARTED!

Oh, all right then, **DO**.

'SO THIS IS HELL. I'D NEVER HAVE BELIEVED IT. YOU REMEMBER ALL WE WERE TOLD ABOUT THE TORTURE CHAMBERS. THE FIRE AND BRIMSTONE...? OLD WIVES' TALES! THERE'S NO NEED FOR RED-HOT POKERS. HELL IS OTHER PEOPLE!'

Jean-Paul Sartre

y-bands. And their managers. Organizatio
like hotels – having 'writers in residence
ompous or what?' In fact, I'm being
ttle hypocritical as I used to be th
Writer in Residence at the TravelMot
odge Inn in West Coventry where I w
he man responsible for writing the bo
opy for the rest ... most popul
arter: Prawn Cocktail tender, plum
tlantic prawns n a bed of cri
eberg lett a cou Ro
uce, garni of lemo
nd present n bread an
utter.' I also he memorab
hrase 'We care the environme
please help us serve energy
-using your tow don't like
past about it. The ession 'Go, girl!'T
orts progra op music as
ackground or spectacul
ies. The nar m-end credits
alf the width een on TV ju
hen you're c k the ca
st. Ads for mo s e.g., 'Col
arrell IS Alex eat'. No he
ot, he's Colin es allowing
lly amou flights so th
ey can eet t ts for promp
ss. For m s f m London
ice take mi and not the tw
ours on the ticke even when th
lane takes off twenty minutes late,
n still arrive on time. TV sports presente
escribing something as 'a big ask
eople calling everyone – even the
hildren – 'mate'. Garbled small 'print'

ANNOYANCE

Charity appeals masquerading as surveys. They don't want to know what we think, they just want our money.

Being served Diet Cola when I order Diet Coke. 'Well, you said you wanted diet and this is diet…' Yes, dummy, Diet *Coke* not Diet *Cola*. Diet Coke is not a generic name for all Diet Colas – especially not the penny-a-glass black piss you've just served me. Just because Diet Coke is a cola does not mean that all colas are Diet Coke. That is a syllogism. But then, if you could understand syllogisms, you'd have been clever enough not to have brought me THE WRONG SODDING DRINK IN THE FIRST PLACE.

On *Countdown*, the continued pretence that the guest personality 'comes up' with words when it's obvious they're being fed them from the gallery.

John Cleese. *Fawlty Towers* was sublime but it was more than thirty years ago. Still thinks he's funny. Alas, he's not.

Being caught talking to myself. Happens more often than I'd like to admit.

Female professional tennis players grunting when they hit the ball. Some of them don't just grunt, they squeal as well – 'ergh-uuuhh!' – like a sow that's enjoying a meal until, suddenly, her favourite piglet is abducted.

Any TV programme with 'house' in the title. Especially *House*.

Scowls from *Big Issue* salesmen when we decide not to buy their magazine. Look, it's very simple, mate. Offer us something we want or need – like an umbrella when it's raining – and we might be interested, but when we've got our hands full of shopping, the last thing we need is something else to carry, like your bloody magazine.

People who tell *Big Issue* sellers to 'get a proper job'. No need: they've been told before.

Seeing someone's face in the mirror behind me while I'm popping a spot.

Goat's cheese. Why?

People who borrow your pen and then suck the top. A plaque on them.

People complaining about the weather in Britain. It's paradise compared to most countries.

The Sainsbury's slogan 'Try Something New Today'. All right, I will. I'll go to Waitrose.

The Lord of The Rings films. I only saw one of them but it was the longest week of my life.

Star rugby league players who move across to rugby union and then fail to live up to expectations.

Local/regional theatre. 'Your all-star cast is headed up by Emmerdale's …'

Fat women in low-slung hipsters. Wear the tents that fat shops thoughtfully provide for you, lard-arses.

The French attitude to infidelity. Mistresses are not uncommon in France. Consider the phrase _cinq à sept_, which is used to signify the hours – between the end of the working day and the return to the family home – when a Frenchman visits his mistress. Such institutionalized immorality really does tell you everything you need to know about the French.

Lost. Appropriate title because I've _Lost_ the will to watch it.

Pistachio nuts that can't be opened.

Health farms. No better than a country house hotel. Without the food.

The Miliband brothers. Both MPs: both weird.

Great singers/actors who give it all up for – yawn – the planet, politics, cat sanctuaries.

Zany comedians. Even if, like Lee Evans, they're incredibly talented.

British heavyweight boxing hopes. They always let us down.

The extraordinarily talented Kate Winslet's attempts to appear normal. You're not, pet, so stop trying.

Shakespeare plays updated and/or set in the wrong period. The only exception being the film of *Richard III* starring Sir Ian McKellen, which was set in the 1930s and was absolutely brilliant.

Men who wear socks with sandals. Should be against the law. It probably is in Italy.

The poor saps who appear in TV ads extolling the virtues of loan companies that have charged them exorbitant rates of interest.

Motorists who park their cars in the car wash and *then* go and buy their ticket – thereby blocking the car wash for those who have already bought theirs.

Graham Norton. He's just Kenneth Williams lite. Very lite.

People who use 'F' instead of 'TH' (as in 'I fink').

TV commercials for nappies.

Manufactured boy-bands. And their managers.

Organizations – like hotels – having 'writers in residence'. Pompous or what? In fact, I'm being a little hypocritical as I used to be the Writer in Residence at the TravelMotorLodgeInn in West Coventry where I was the man responsible for writing the body copy for the restaurant's most popular starter: Prawn Cocktail. 'Tender, plump Atlantic prawns nestling on a bed of crisp iceberg lettuce in our own Marie Rose sauce, garnished with a twist of lemon and presented with brown bread and butter.' I also created the memorable phrase 'We care about the environment so please help us to conserve energy by re-using your towels' but I don't like to boast about it.

The expression 'Go, girl!'

TV sports programmes using pop music as a background to great goals or spectacular tries.

The narrowing of film-end credits to half the width of the screen on TV just when you're trying to check the cast list.

Ads for movies that say, e.g., 'Colin Farrell IS Alexander the Great'. No he's not, he's Colin Farrell.

People who choose anything other than 'ordinary' names for their children. This applies particularly to daughters. My advice to prospective parents is to go into any city-central public phone-box and rule out the names on all the cards they find there. I'm not an expert, you understand, but this would exclude Tiffany, Jade, Amber, Kelly and Honey.

Names people have given their children:
(and expect us not to laugh)

Moon Unit, Dweezil, Diva & Emuukha Rodan – Frank Zappa.

Dandelion (now Angela) – Keith Richards.

Dog – Sky Saxon.

Camera – Arthur Ashe.

Zowie (now Joey) – David Bowie.

Sailor – Christie Brinkley.

Phoenix – Mel B.

Free – Barbara Hershey & David Carradine.

Blue Angel – The Edge.

Gulliver – Gary Oldman.

Justice – Steven Seagal.

Sage Moonblood – Sylvester Stallone.

True, Ocean & **Sonnet** – Forest Whitaker.

Chance – Larry King.

Speck Wildhorse – John Cougar Mellencamp.

Lennon – Liam Gallagher & Patsy Kensit.

Pixie, Fifi Trixiebelle & **Peaches** – Bob Geldof & Paula Yates.

Heavenly Hiraani Tigerlily – Michael Hutchence & Paula Yates.

Happy – Macy Gray.

Denim – Toni Braxton.

Jermajesty – Jermaine Jackson.

Pilot Inspektor Riesgraf Lee – Jason Lee

Tu – Rob Morrow (Tu Morrow… geddit?)

Audio Science Sossamon – Shannon Sossamon

Geronimo – Alex James.

Apple – Gwyneth Paltrow & Chris Martin.

Seven – Erykah Badu.

Kal-el (Superman's real name) – Nicolas Cage.

Bluebell Madonna – Geri Halliwell.

Dusti Rain & **KeeLee Breeze** – Vanilla Ice.

Airlines allowing a silly amount of time for flights so that they can meet their targets for promptness. For example, flights from London to Nice take ninety minutes and not the two hours on the ticket. So even when the plane takes off twenty minutes late, it can still arrive on time.

TV sports presenters describing something as 'a big ask'.

People calling everyone – even their children – 'mate'.

Garbled small 'print' in radio ads.

Out-of-date posters for fetes and plays still adorning lampposts.

Postmodernism. Whatever it is.

Post-irony. No such thing.

The word 'executive' used to flog poky flats.

Five-a-day coordinators. Let them eat cake.

Radio ads extolling the benefits of radio advertising.

People driving 4x4s when they're never going to go off-road.

Loud music in pubs inhibiting any conversation.

Supermarkets calling themselves *your* Safeway/Waitrose/ Tesco etc.

Unnecessary apostrophe's.

People who list silly hobbies – like sleeping – in *Who's Who*.

'Loved up' (qv) couples talking to each other in baby talk and addressing each other by pet names – usually extremely embarrassing ones – in company. Save it for the bedroom, 'bears'.

'Loved up' (qv) couples feeding each other in restaurants. And, worse still, breaking off from feeding each other to kiss.

'Loved up' (qv) couples who boast about buying cuddly toys for each other.

'Loved up' (qv) couples who boast about buying cuddly toys for each other. And tell you the cuddly toys' names.

'Loved up' (qv) couples who boast about buying cuddly toys for each other. And tell you the cuddly toys' names. And alert you to the cuddly toys' birthdays.

People who ring up when you're very busy, and say, 'Guess who this is …'

The word 'drawing' pronounced as 'drawring'.

Wasps. Totally unnecessary. Unlike bees.

Stores playing 'Jingle Bells' in October.

Anyone under the age of forty who writes their autobiography.

Being told to 'listen up' as opposed to being asked to 'listen'.

People who say 'in my humble opinion'. The humility is never genuine.

Being asked whether we've got loyalty/reward cards in shops after we've spent less than a fiver.

Newspapers adding 'gate' to any and every scandal.

Products that boast of expensive ingredients when those ingredients make up about 2 per cent of the total content.

TV continuity announcers' fake enthusiasm when promoting truly awful shows.

Artificially whitened teeth (very scary).

Ex-professional sportsmen criticizing current ones. 'In my day …'

TV ads for ear-wax softeners. Even worse when we're eating.

Ladettes.

Prince Harry. So like his father…

Doughnuts sold as 'donuts'.

Clothing with big logos. It's just free advertising.

The use in shop names/signs of U instead of 'you' and R instead of 'are'.

DEAL OR NO DEAL PEEVES

Contestants who milk their moment of glory for all it's worth.

Noel Edmonds saying 'You will come back' before a break in *Deal Or No Deal* (the trouble is, we do).

The jargon: the Power Five, the Banker's Power Five, the Crazy Chair, the Dream Factory, the East/West Wings, Eight-board, Pilgrims.

The Banker offering less than the average of the remaining boxes (and still being thanked for his generosity).

Noel Edmonds telling people to 'concentrate' and 'stay focused'. Why? They're only picking boxes at random.

People saying 'Good luck' as they open the boxes. (Let's take it as read, shall we?)

People saying they've got a strong feeling what's inside their box. Almost invariably wrong.

Pathetic attempts at spontaneity.

Tactics – as if…

Personnel departments renamed Human Resources.

Celebrities describing themselves as Buddhists on the strength of something they once read in a glossy magazine article.

People who make a big thing of how much they hate their feet. Is that *really* the worst thing about you?

TV game-show contestants who clap themselves. They look like seals.

Aromatherapy/aromatherapists. Essential oils, eh? Essential? How essential would that be then? Not very essential at all, if you really think about it. So that leaves the massage, which is as good as the person giving it. And if that person is calling himself or herself an aromatherapist, then it probably won't be as good as the one you'd get off an ordinary masseur/masseuse.

Grown-ups wearing braces on their teeth.

Colin Firth's moody acting style. Though I suspect that the genders might divide on this one.

People – especially sportsmen – who offer to give more than 100 per cent.

Motorcyclists weaving through traffic and relying on car drivers' alertness and forbearance. But I'm only jealous because I no longer have a moped to get through central London.

The use of the expression 'to go' instead of 'takeaway'.

Being told that I bite my nails badly when, in fact, I bite them bloody well.

Men who wear very obvious wigs or toupees.

The words 'New & Improved' on products. If it's new it can't be improved.

Once-beautiful female TV presenters complaining that women are only hired for their looks.

The Great Escape Oh, don't get me wrong, it's a fabulous film – even on the hundredth viewing, but there are so many things about it that make me angry. For example: if everyone knows that Richard Attenborough is Big X, why do they bother to give him a codename? Given that there are Americans in the camp, how come James Coburn is cast as an Australian? Isn't there a kinder way to point out Donald Pleasance's myopia rather than tripping him up? And given that he was so short-sighted, why did he go out for that joyride in the first place? If Steve McQueen can escape underneath the wire so easily, why do they bother digging a tunnel? And how come McQueen is allowed to wear sixties casual clothing? Why does Charles Bronson try to join the Russian POWs at the start of the film? And finally, why oh why does Gordon Jackson always fall for the old trick of answering in English when the Gestapo man tells him to have a pleasant journey?

ANNOYANCE

Dame Cleo Laine's voice. Goes straight through me and I don't mean that as a compliment.

Sadie Frost. Not as pretty as her ex.

TV advertisements for feminine hygiene products. You know what I mean.

The euphemisms employed in TV advertisements for feminine hygiene products.

All footballers being called 'football stars' rather than footballers in news stories. It might make the stories more exciting but it's still annoying when the player in question has only played a few first-team games for his club.

The expression 'It's not rocket science'. What if it is?

People who care what brand of mineral water they're drinking. They wouldn't be able to identify it in a blind tasting, the idiots: it's all in the packaging.

TV newsreaders standing up.

Goatee beards. They're a sign of *something* not quite right.

Discovering that almost everything we eat, drink and breathe is ultimately bad for us. Serves us right for reading the papers, I guess.

Supermarket cashiers chatting with customers when there are other people waiting to be served.

Having an unfashionable ailment. I suffer from gout. Everyone treats it as a joke or as a self-inflicted wound. 'Been drinking too much port!' people say to me, laughing as though they weren't the zillionth person to have cracked that gag. In fact, gout is a hereditary condition precipitated by an excess of uric acid which is exacerbated not by port but by offal (something that I loathe). When attacks occur they are unbelievably painful – worse than childbirth, according to women who've experienced both – and yet there are no self-help groups, no 'Buddies' and absolutely no charity rock concerts.

The scrapping of Concorde. I never flew on it but it felt good to know it was there.

The National Anthem. Ghastly. Princess Anne is absolutely right: we should replace it with *Land of Hope And Glory*.

TV soap characters saying, 'We've got to talk.' As opposed to?

Silly car number plates that don't quite manage to spell out the names of the idiots who bought them.

UPVC double-glazing installed in old houses.

People who play – or try to play – poker because it's trendy.

MCs asking audiences to 'Give it up for…' Whatever happened to 'Give a big hand to…'?

People who send Christmas cards when it's too late for you to send one back – especially tricky for those of us who employ a purely defensive strategy to such things.

Very short powerful men married to very tall beautiful women. E.g. Bernie Ecclestone.

TV ads for air fresheners. Especially the one featuring an infant sitting on a potty.

Jews for Jesus – it's like Arsenal supporters for Spurs.

People who press 'Reply to All' when they're responding to jokey emails. You're not as funny as you think you are, you know.

All-white girl singing groups. Always disappointing.

Rugby Union stars who become famous outside of the sport: Gavin Henson, Kyran Bracken, Matt Dawson. All, I'm sure, fine men. but it goes against the spirit of Rugby Union.

Too-mellow late-night DJs.

The expression, 'Fair play to …' Where did that come from?

Puns. Unless they're really clever. Compulsive punsters are scary: it's real punography.

Any man who refers to his wife as ''er indoors'. Except Arthur Daley of course.

Tara Palmer-Tomkinson. I met her before she was famous. We were introduced by a mutual friend. I asked her what she did for a living. 'I'm a model,' she purred with so much haughty arrogance that I couldn't resist replying: 'Only just.' She walked off in a huff. Anyway, her name is an anagram of I AM A PLONKER – NOT SMART. I rest my case.

People who make visitors to their homes remove their shoes at the front door.

Hugh Hefner. Although he's somewhere between 80 and dead, he's still getting more action than I am.

Nicky Campbell. Too pleased with himself – by a long chalk.

Overly camp TV presenters.

TV holiday programmes. Why do the presenters never miss their flights or turn up at half-finished hotels?

TIMESHARE COMPANIES:
What They Say … And What They Really Mean

'Have you thought about a holiday investment?'
(Who said anything about 'timeshare'?)

'Congratulations, you have been chosen…'
(That's right, we bought your name on a mailing list.)

'Enjoy free holidays for the rest of your life.'
(Free except for the four-figure service charges.)

'Buy now at this unbelievable price.'
(Yup, even we can't believe we're charging so much.)

'You have won either a car, a new home or a £100 voucher off our guaranteed property bond.'
(Well, which one do you think you're going to get?)

'Don't forget there's a cooling-off period.'
(Not if you read the small print.)

'Do you want a lucky scratchcard?'
(Any prize you like so long as it's a glass of sherry at a four-hour hard sell.)

'Exclusive location.'
(Even the Spanish planning authorities didn't know it could be developed.)

'Low season.' (It's so quiet even the staff are on holiday.)

'There's a free taxi from your hotel to the presentation.'
(Enjoy the walk back if you don't sign up.)

The Antiques Roadshow. The greed, the greed.

Beautiful celebrities claiming that they were ugly children. Yeah, we know, nobody ever thought you were beautiful and that explains why you can't get enough of it now but please, do us a favour, save it for your therapist.

Footballers taking their shirts off after scoring goals. Why?

Men who claim to share the housework with their wives. Sorry to let the side down but I don't believe it. All those years of consciousness-raising haven't produced 'new men' but 'crafty chaps'. They – all right, 'we' – now know better than to refuse to participate in what our fathers would have called 'women's work' so, instead, we make all the right noises and do just enough to get away without censure. You'll recognize the sort of man I'm talking about: he's the one doing a lap of honour round the living room just because he changed a nappy. And you can be sure it was only a wet one.

Reality TV shows.

Reality TV show 'stars'.

People who read over our shoulders on trains and buses.

'Funny' answering-machine messages that aren't.

The sort of CDs sold by supermarkets – tiny choice; all ghastly.

25

The word 'Hello!?' used to mean 'Excuse me'.

Sports' pundits inability to speak proper English. Almost all of them – irrespective of the sport – eschew adverbs. We'd settle for the boy done well instead of the boy done great.

Smoking motorists who use the road as an ashtray.

TV channels that run the news in the middle of feature films.

People who use the word 'angst' instead of 'anxiety'.

Any man who calls himself a film-maker – unless he earns a living solely from film-making.

Trumpets in the crowd at England soccer matches.

TV ads for anti-wrinkle creams presented by young models.

Ludicrous names for paint colours. Portia for peach; Reverie for light peach; Candesse for even lighter peach. No need to dress them up: we're grown-ups – we can take it straight.

Traditional folk music. Men in hand-knitted chunky jumpers trying to rid their ears of wax.

Makeover TV programmes. I can see what's in it for the participant(s), but what's in it for us?

Food labelled as 'natural' when it's obvious that it is.

Nude charity calendars. No cause is worth being exposed to a sixty-year-old woman's droopy tits.

Food labelled as 'natural' when it's obvious that it isn't.

Pubs that advertise things happening TONITE.

The euphemism 'gentle comedy' used to describe mirthless programmes – e.g. *Keeping Up Appearances, Last of The Summer Wine.* What did they give those studio audiences to make them laugh like that? It sure as hell wasn't funny lines.

The expression 24/7. Actually, not the expression so much as the people who use it.

TV presenters who wear bow-ties in an attempt to become 'personalities'. Apparently, it is a sign of a very small penis.

Razor-blade manufacturers adding yet *more* blades.

Other people's litter in stacked supermarket trolleys.

Motorists who neglect to thank us when we've let them out of a side turning.

Young men who plaster hair gel on their hair to make it stupidly spiky.

Thirty-something women going on about their 'biological clocks'. I'm a happily married man so I hear you ticking but I can't come in.

Ski bores.

Annoying things skiers say:

'We found a wonderful resort where there were absolutely no queues.'

'I can't believe that anyone could dislike skiing.'

'There's nothing better than a hot bath after a hard day's skiing.'

'I think you just have to buy your own skis.'

'Of course, I don't bother with the après-ski.'

'I hate it when the snow's too powdery.'

'I don't think three holidays a year is overdoing it.'

'You can't beat skiing off-piste.'

'I regard the money I spend on my equipment as an investment.'

'Oh it was great, we played Trivial Pursuit every night!'

Titles ten minutes into feature films.

Bald (male) celebrities who wear hats indoors.

Travel brochures with prices *from*...

TV programmes on interior design.

Actors releasing records. Always a dumb idea.

Novelty toilet signs in theme pubs that leave you confused as to which one you're supposed to use.

People who say 'at this moment in time...' instead of 'now'.

Home-owners boasting about how much their property has gone up in value. We all do it but that doesn't make it any more palatable.

TV game-show contestants name-checking the host at the end of every answer.

People who use toothpicks in public. When did that become acceptable?

Thirty-something female newspaper journalists who universalize their own lives. 'Have you noticed how everyone's pregnant at the moment? At my toddler's playgroup, almost half the mothers are expecting and *all* my friends in the NCT group are pregnant...'

Celebrity umpires/referees. Remain anonymous please.

The members of the Academy of Motion Pictures for denying Oscars to Gene Kelly, Cary Grant, James Mason, Greta Garbo, Judy Garland and Sir Dirk Bogarde (who was never even nominated).

People who say 'no problem' when you thank them for a gift.

Nobodies being referred to as 'icons'.

Celebrity hairdressers. We could live without them, I think.

Men wearing bling. A wristwatch is quite sufficient for any man. Oh, all right, and a simple wedding ring if it's an absolute necessity. Anything more is just wrong. Look, rappers wear bling and rappers get shot: a syllogism? I do hope not.

Men with high-pitched voices. Scary.

Mnemonics that are harder to remember than the things they're designed to make easier (e.g. the countries of Central America in geographical order – Belize, Guatemala, Honduras, Nicaragua, Costa Rica, Panama – BeeGee's Hen! Se 'er pee?).

The expression 'meaningful dialogue'. Isn't that just a conversation?

People who can eat what they like without putting on weight.

Packets of roast-chicken-flavoured crisps labelled 'Suitable for vegetarians'. Annoyingly confusing.

Anyone who's not Scottish saying 'wee' instead of 'little'.

The use of a 'z' instead of an 's' in company or product names – e.g. Kidz.

Staplers that run out of staples when you have just one thing to staple.

People saying that a record sounds as good/fresh as the day it was recorded. Er, obviously it does: it's a record, that's the point.

Postmen being called 'posties'.

Adults who boast about reading children's books (e.g. Harry Potter).

Our favourite foods being the most fattening.

People who say 'burgalry' instead of burglary.

DVD extras. We just feel guilty for not watching them.

Antique shops and tea shops which spell 'old' with an e at the end.

Ethical investment funds – or rather the smug bastards who buy them. What I want is a nice fat juicy

ANNOYANCE

unethical investment fund that'll give me the money that Gordon Brown stole from me when he was Chancellor.

Any man who says 'It's from the heart'. He's almost certainly trying to get laid, the bastard.

Wild mushrooms. Much better tamed.

Computers that do what you tell them to do – not what you *want* them to do.

Otherwise intelligent people who become helpless as soon as they sit in front of a computer screen.

Genuine IT Helpdesk Query

Customer: My keyboard is not working.

Helpdesk: Are you sure it's plugged into the computer?

Customer: No. I can't get behind the computer.

Helpdesk: Pick up your keyboard and walk 10 paces back.

Customer: OK.

Helpdesk: Did the keyboard come with you?

Customer: Yes.

Helpdesk: That means the keyboard is not plugged in.

People who don't complete the round. On a regular basis. We know who you are and we're just biding our time.

People who hire stretch limos so that other people will think they're celebrities. We don't.

Men with leather elbow patches on their jackets or jumpers. Unless, I guess, they're teachers.

Cinemas that insist on showing only children's films in the school holidays.

The small bits of cotton that hold new pairs of socks together.

People who pay compliments like they expect receipts.

Any newspaper article that begins with the word 'So...'

Internet forums. Very rarely worth the visit.

People who own a silly number of pairs of trainers. Someone called Goldie apparently owns more than 1,600 while Damon Dash – whoever he is – is said to have three thousand. Then there's P. Diddy (qv) who throws his away after wearing them for just one day.

That American bloke with the unfeasibly deep voice who seems to do the cinema trailer for every film – even British films set in Britain.

Friends who turn out to be flaky. Friends help you move. Real friends help you move bodies.

People who use Latin expressions like 'per se' and 'ipso facto'.

People who misuse Latin expressions like 'per se' and 'ipso facto'.

War gamers. There is a very fine line between 'hobby' and 'mental illness'.

Other comics knocking Ben Elton for working with Sir Andrew Lloyd Webber and Queen. OK, so they're not my faves either but at least Ben doesn't do commercials like so many of his detractors do.

The apparently mandatory use of the word 'pamper' or 'pampering' in any newspaper write-up of a spa.

Pimped-up cars.

Tasteless faux-rustic ornamental tat peddled by tacky souvenir shops in 'picture postcard' twee villages and downmarket seaside resorts.

Comedy T-shirts (e.g. Genius When Drunk).

Plate-smashing in Greek restaurants. Now in a *French* restaurant…

Vending machines/car-parking machines that don't dispense change.

Baseball caps worn indoors.

People who think that Elvis is still alive. He's not. No, honestly, he's not.

Gossips – but not necessarily gossip.

Men who don't move their arms when they walk. Sure sign of weirdness.

Tartan coats on small dogs.

The knowledge that our computers are horribly out of date even before they're delivered.

People who say 'Only in America!' after hearing a story about America. They've invariably never even been there.

People who clearly don't exercise wearing trainers and tracksuits.

The TV ads for Sheilas' Wheels (if only the jingle weren't so catchy).

Young people who, er, like, misuse the word 'like' several times in conversation.

Bald men with ponytails.

Continual repeats of *Only Fools and Horses* on BBC TV. It was never as good as *Minder* in the first place.

The use of the word 'aqua' on beauty products in an attempt to mask the fact that the product is nine-tenths water.

Supermarket reward cards. Just cut the prices please. Even so, it's still irksome when we find ourselves in a supermarket for which we don't have the appropriate reward card.

Having to sit through advertisements in the cinema (it doesn't happen in the US).

Things being described as 'the new black'.

Clowns. Very strange.

People in bare feet in TV furniture ads.

Radio DJs who talk over the intros to records.

The word co-worker. What's wrong with colleague?

Identical identikit town centres throughout the country. Obviates the incentive to leave your own town.

People who call rugby 'rugger'. The reason for this, as I explained in *Why Girls Can't Throw*, which is available in all good bookshops (qv), is because in the late 19th century, public school and Oxbridge boys had a mania for putting an -er on the end of words – as a form of slang. So just as breakfast became 'brekker', Association Football became 'soccer' – or, worse, 'footer' – and Rugby Football 'rugger'. And, because these fellows controlled the sport for many years, it stuck. Still doesn't make it any more acceptable.

THE LAWS OF BBQS

The more lighter fuel you use to get the barbecue going, the more likely you are to run out of matches.

The people who bring supermarket hamburgers always cook themselves steaks.

Any barbecue to which you invite more than six people will be washed out by rain.

The smoke from the barbecue can be guaranteed to waft into the garden of your least neighbourly neighbour.

The more gaudy the apron worn by the man doing the barbecue, the less likely it is that the meat will be cooked through properly.

It is impossible to toast hamburger buns on the barbecue without burning them.

The barbecue only really gets hot once all the food has been cooked.

The chicken is always scarily undercooked.

If there aren't enough sausages to go around, the last one can always be guaranteed to fall on to the coals.

All other men attending will offer their (unwanted) advice on best barbecue techniques.

It is invariably a man who cooks on the barbecue.

It is invariably a woman who cleans up the barbecue.

American settings and accents in ads for British products.

People who read papers and magazines in newsagents without paying for them. Sad, sad, sad.

People who say 'uzz' instead of 'us'.

Trendy, expensive clothes made poorly.

Jordan & Peter. Weren't two enormously useless tits enough for her?

Gail Porter. What Susan Hampshire was to dyslexia, Gail Porter is to alopecia. Get yourself a wig, girl, and get over it.

People who keep plastic covers on their car seats and, worse, on their three-piece suites.

Pundits and sportswriters who call football 'the beautiful game'.

Waiters/waitresses who ask if everything's OK just as you've put a forkful in your mouth.

Throwing away junk that has been hoarded for years – just a few days before we need it.

Non-Australians saying 'No worries'.

Having to negotiate aisles of beauty counters every time we enter a department store.

Book covers on which the author's name is bigger than the title.

Davina McCall. Can't see it myself.

Tuna being referred to as 'tuna-fish'. No other fish suffers this fate.

Ice-cream headaches. Ouch.

The expression 'What are you like!' used as a statement and not as a question.

Soap-opera bores. Get a life.

The design of our bodies. For example: having arms too short to scratch the middle of our backs.

Email 'emoticons' – especially smileys. Forgivable (just) on a nine-year-old girl's emails but utterly wrong when used by ANYONE else.

International Rugby Union players wearing bus conductresses' gloves.

People who eat while they're on the phone to us.

Footballers' girlfriends who call themselves 'models' when they're not.

Celebrity couples who play out their relationships in the public eye, and the sugary words *Hello!* magazine employs to describe celebrity relationships.

Ten Stages in a Relationship as Reported in *Hello!*

1. So Happy: Janet And John Reveal Their Whirlwind Romance.

2. John Talks For The First Time About His Love For Janet As They Announce Their Engagement.

3. Sunshine And Smiles: Exclusive Photographs Of Janet And John's Star-studded Wedding.

4. Janet And John Invite Us In To Their Sumptuous Home And Tell Us How Their Love Has Grown From Strength To Strength In The Past Six Weeks.

5. Janet Talks To Us Of Her Joy At The Thought Of Becoming A Mother For The First Time.

6. Janet And John Introduce Us To Their Four-day-old Son, Tarquin.

7. On Holiday With Janet And John As They Dismiss Rumours Of Marital Difficulties.

8. The Sad Story Behind The Break-up Of Janet And John.

9. John Tells Us Of His Sorrow As He Loses Battle To Keep His Children.

10. Janet Introduces Us To David And Tells Us How She's Found Happiness At Last.

Being asked by anyone who's not Irish, 'How's yourself, then?'

Limited-edition chocolate bars. They're not paintings, you know.

Retired people who say: 'I don't know how I ever found time to go out to work.' Yawn.

Obvious straggly hair extensions.

Dentists filling our mouths with instruments and swabs and then asking us questions about our holiday plans.

People who use deodorants instead of washing. Lynx and BO isn't a particularly edifying combo.

In hotels, having to smile at people before breakfast.

People who start sentences with the preamble, 'Don't get me wrong, but...'

Americans calling toilets 'restrooms'. No one goes to the bog to 'rest' (though those of us with irritable bowels might very well go there to 'toil').

Channel 4 Best of/Worst of programmes.

The pundits they use on Channel 4 Best of/Worst of programmes.

Low-calorie salad dressings. All vile.

THINGS THAT PARENTS DO TO EMBARRASS THEIR CHILDREN

Call children's friends by their nicknames.

Insist on using catchphrases from *Little Britain*.

Insist on dancing at their children's parties.

Stand at the door and call out 'Good luck!' as they go off on a date.

Refuse to take part in the parents' race on sports day.

Take part in the parents' race on sports day.

Ask if they've finished their homework as they're about to go out with their friends.

Persist in calling the weekly allowance 'pocket money' – especially in company.

Kiss them effusively in public.

Show baby pictures to their children's boyfriends/girlfriends.

Make references to the fact that they (the parents) are still sexually active.

THINGS THAT CHILDREN DO TO EMBARRASS THEIR PARENTS

Reveal Mum and Dad's pet names for each other.

Lead the chorus of laughter when their parents attempt to do anything sporty.

Refuse to wear the right clothes for (extended) family gatherings.

Swear in front of elderly relatives.

Repeat parental rows verbatim to third parties.

Refuse to introduce them to their friends.

Remind them what they really think of someone in front of that person.

Say 'Mum and Dad say we're too poor to have a holiday this year' just as their parents are trying to impress someone.

Laugh when their parents kiss.

Newspaper articles that start with the 'jokey' words: 'It's official!'

Price rhetoric – goods priced at, say, £19.99 instead of £20.

The word 'invite' used as a noun instead of 'invitation'.

Local traffic reports breaking on to our car radios to tell us that the roads are clear and there are no problems.

The overuse of the words amazing, brilliant, unbelievable and fantastic.

Guest speakers introduced with the words, 'Without further ado'.

Reporters who wave their hands about when they talk.

Predictive text. No, I can't do it either.

Metrosexuality. Not entirely sure what it is but I don't think I like the sound of it.

Famous actors doing voiceover work that really ought to be done by their struggling fellow thesps.

People who *always* say 'Absolutely!' or 'Definitely!' instead of yes.

People who don't understand coincidence. I was walking down the street the other day, thinking about my old friend Jonathan – and guess what? I didn't bump into him. Another friend was playing golf and didn't score a hole-in-one. Neither did his father who was playing on a different course at a slightly later time. My grandfather died in 1971. My grandmother died 17 years 112 days later. So what?

So what indeed.

Look, obviously coincidences happen and, when they do, we notice them. We talk about them to our friends, we embellish them (the person we met on holiday who coincidentally lived in the same street eventually mutates into our next-door neighbour). Why? Because we want to bring meaning and order – or synchronicity as Jung called it – to our lives and also because coincidences are, as G.K. Chesterton said, 'spiritual puns'. So far, no harm done.

The trouble is all those people who think that any coincidence is part of some kind of giant plan/psychic phenomenon/evidence of God/fate/karma.

It's just coincidence and it would be a coincidence if there were never any coincidences. So just accept it, dummies.

Tiny print on packets of food. What are they trying to hide?

Enemies from our schooldays who are richer and more successful than us.

Friends from our schooldays who are richer and more successful than us.

'DAYS'

Some are daft but harmless – like National Sleep-in Day, National Stick The Kettle On Day, Wet Nose Day, National Escargot Day, Random Huggers Day, National Masturbation Day (I kid you not), National Day of Courtesy, National Thank You Day, World Kindness Day, World Toilet Day (phew, that's a relief), World Turtle Day, National Impotence Day (no thanks), World Smile Day, World Naturist Day, International Aperitif Day, International Tampon Alert Day, National Bug-busting Day, National Kissing Day (presumably doesn't coincide with National Masturbation Day), World Pole Dancing Day (presumably does), National Hot Dog Day (with a day off the next day on which to recover?), International Talk Like A Pirate Day, National Erotica Day.

Trouble with so many of these days is that they encourage the office clown to be even more of a twat than usual.

Others are a lot more sinister: International Car Free Day, Earth Day, Europe Day, World Debt Day, Buy Nothing Day, World Anti-McDonald's Day (you'd have thought that for the sort of people who'll observe this 'Day', *every* day is Anti-McDonald's Day).

Mistaking battered squid for onion rings. Unnerving for those of us who like the latter but detest the former.

Golf commentators who call Colin Montgomerie 'Muntgumerie'. The conts.

The number of production companies listed at the start of modern films. Try counting 'em.

Park & Ride schemes. Defeats the whole point of driving a car.

People who say 'inferring' when they mean 'implying'.

People who say 'implying' when they mean 'inferring'.

Christians who put fish symbols on their cars and then don't let me out into the traffic. (Not very Christian, is it?)

People in native costumes being presented to royalty. It's like presenting pearly kings and queens to foreign dignitaries.

The logo for the 2012 Olympics. Pathetic.

People who go on about how awful the logo for the 2012 Olympics is. Even more pathetic.

'A LIFETIME OF HAPPINESS!
NO MAN ALIVE COULD BEAR IT:
IT WOULD BE HELL ON EARTH.'

George Bernard Shaw

e North (or East, West etc.). You'll no
at Venice doesn't call itself the Birmin
am of the South. The televised auditi
ound of shows like Britain's Got Tale
's kicking cripples. Contestants in su
hows whingeing about how cruel t
dges were. Hadn't they seen past serie
oud music played (just) under the ne
eadlines.The use of American (rath
han English) sp ngs   o us a fav
dolescents we   doub
iscount sofa   claim
yummy yummy   proclai
g it ma es it   toilet ro
her   e sheet   half
   eel   of syn   nea
nish   Men   their   ea
ut you whe   oo   who
ght b   the swe packe
hrough   movi
n' as   someon
ermetically c ne   and therefo
nopenable   cts.Men's trouse
nd shorts   baggy pocke
alfway   s.People w
escrib   life confiden
he   o   ds – like t
ning of a   th – in foods li
eel C   stmas p ding that cou
nd s   be suitable r vegetaria
nternet d   g sites. On   gly people a
nline now .'For sure' used where 'y
ould suffice. Drivers who think
azard warning lights render their
nvisible.Any man who makes a big d
f his birthday.Women with more

AGGRAVATION

Restaurants that fill Heinz Tomato Ketchup bottles with a cheap and nasty generic brand.

Female sports reporters. Never convincing – even when they're ugly.

Junk mail that disguises itself as proper mail. 'Private and confidential: this requires your immediate attention.' No it's not; no it doesn't.

The use of the word 'proactive'.

People who say, 'You can do mine afterwards!' when you're cleaning your car. In fact, make that *anyone* who (effectively) puts an exclamation mark at the end of their sentences.

The expression 'It'll all come out in the wash'. Not blood, you platitudinous sod.

Slim women in TV ads moaning about feeling bloated. Oh dear, how sad, never mind.

People who start sentences with the expression, 'I'm not a prude but…' To deny it is to affirm it.

Life insurance companies offering us M&S vouchers if we buy policies. We'll buy products on merit, thank you, we don't need to be bribed.

Foreigners in English football. The national side loses every tournament it plays in: some connection surely?

Fat Elvis Presley impersonators. Always wearing those horrible white jumpsuits. You never see men impersonating the young gorgeous Elvis.

People who pronounce 'new' as 'noo'. Only permissible from native New Yorkers.

TV companies interrupting the end of programmes to give details of forthcoming programmes.

Having to buy packs of four batteries for gadgets that require only two.

Rubberneckers posing and gesturing behind TV presenters doing pieces to camera.

24-hour rolling TV news. Either it's not really news or you end up watching the same sodding items half a dozen times an hour.

Pubs offering 'Home-cooked Food'. We can get that at home. We go out for professionally cooked food.

People who have mobile phones but then boast that they don't use them. And the point is …?

That appallingly common man who always seems to be on morning TV helping people to buy houses. Can't be bothered to find out who he is.

The use of the word 'comforted' to describe what Celebrity A is doing to Celebrity B who has just split up from Celebrity C.

Moving news bars on satellite TV news channels. How are we men supposed to concentrate on two things at once?

Other people's tuneless whistling.

Conservative politicians trying to sound 'street'. Impossible.

Answering machines that cut us off before we've finished speaking.

People who say 'end of' to terminate a conversation.

The advertising slogan 'We Live Electricals!'

Aristocrats who complain about being poor when the sale of one of their many paintings would leave them comfortable for the rest of their worthless lives.

Football clubs changing their kit to make more money out of their fans.

Football fans who grumble about ever-changing replica shirts and then buy them anyway.

Parking in an empty car park and coming back to find that the only other person to park after you, parks so close to your car that you can't open the door.

The self-aggrandizing use of the word 'project' instead of the words 'task' or 'job'.

Any politician who claims to like the Arctic Monkeys.

The use of the word 'amount' instead of 'number' when talking about people.

Television schedulers who cut off the credits at the end of old films.

Proms and yearbooks in British secondary schools.

The use of the word 'creative' applied to men with ponytails who work in advertising.

Middle-aged males who try to enhance their image by not shaving for two days.

Ice cream that is too hard to scoop out. We don't appreciate expending calories when we're of a mind to indulge ourselves.

Non-stick cookware which sticks after it's been used a few times.

Being told that doing nothing is not an option. Usually it is.

Feng-shui. All tosh. Who'd have thought people could be so gullible?

Hollywood actors in West End plays.

The same TV trails endlessly repeated.

People who walk off zebra crossings at an angle, making you wait even longer for them to reach the other side.

Fast-food chains trying to pass off their fat-laden food as healthy by adding a bit of lettuce and a slice of tomato.

Supermarket colas. All rank. No exceptions.

Yellow ribbons.

The Osbournes. I don't get it – or is that the point?

Shop assistants chewing gum.

55

Places calling themselves the Venice of the North (or East, West etc.). You'll note that Venice doesn't call itself the Birmingham of the South.

The televised audition round of shows like *Britain's Got Talent*. It's kicking cripples.

Contestants in such shows whingeing about how cruel the judges were. Hadn't they seen past series?

Loud music played (just) under the news headlines.

The use of American (rather than English) spellings. Do us a favor.

Adolescents wearing hoodies.

Double-discount-sofa TV ads.

Self-proclaimed 'yummy mummies'. The act of proclaiming it makes it not so.

Two-ply toilet rolls where the sheet perforations are half a sheet out of sync until the roll is nearly finished.

Men who shave their heads but not their faces.

Cinemagoers who sit right behind us and rustle sweet packets throughout the film.

The expression 'moving on' as a euphemism for dumping someone.

Hermetically cellophaned – and therefore unopenable – products.

Men's trousers and shorts with huge, baggy pockets halfway down the legs.

People who describe themselves as 'life confident'.

WIMBLEDON
The Only Ways in which We Brits Triumph

Receiving the most wild-card entries.

Cheering giant TV screens.

Quaffing Champagne in hospitality tents.

Queuing.

Having the most humourless officials in the world.

Charging over the odds for strawberries.

Rain commentaries.

Accepting dodgy line calls.

Losing gracefully.

Ticket-touting.

The use of animal products – like the lining of a cow's stomach – in foods like cheese or Christmas pudding that could (and should) be suitable for vegetarians.

Internet dating sites. Only ugly people are 'online now'.

'For sure' used where 'yes' would suffice.

Drivers who think that hazard warning lights render their cars invisible.

Any man who makes a big deal of his birthday.

Women with more male than female friends (and vice-versa). Not to be trusted.

Humourless people who use your humour in evidence against you.

Having to work when the weather's bad. (See also page 167.)

Being told, 'You think *you've* got problems…'

People who say 'you know' every four or five words.

Men who wear scarves indoors.

Not being sure whether it's scarves or scarfs.

The automatic assumption that all pensioners are frail and/or senile. Just as bad as the pretension that all pensioners are go-getting fit silver surfers.

People who say 'pass' when asked a question to which they don't know the answer.

Anyone who refers to *Coronation Street* as 'Corrie'.

The expression 'not many' used to mean 'yes'.

Badly spoken children's TV presenters.

People who tell you to 'get a life' or 'get out more'. They're really talking to themselves (or ought to be).

People making fun of people with ginger hair. The last unprotected minority.

Vapid TV presenters who yearn to show us more of their inner selves. Difficult to do when you don't actually have an inner self.

Jonathan (but not David) Dimbleby. How pleased with himself can a man be?

People who pride themselves on their frankness. Not always so ready to accommodate other people's frankness. See Prince Philip (qv).

Anyone who claims that they attended 'the university of life'. The only possible retort is: 'Pity you didn't graduate.'

Professional Jocks – like Sir Sean Connery – who bang on about independence for a country they choose not to live in (see also Professional Scousers and Professional Tykes).

TV drama documentaries that distort the truth.

Ex-celebrities doing satellite TV commercials for wrinkly pension plans. Complete with grisly references to 'those FINAL expenses'.

Film reviews that give away the plot.

People who boast that they never read. Not much of a boast, is it? And as Twain said, 'The person who can read but doesn't is no better off than a man who can't read at all.'

Pub and restaurant gardens. The law of unintended consequences means that as a result of the smoking ban, these prime spots are now totally full and/or fuggy with smoke.

The people who go on *Trisha*. But not Trisha.

The expression 'Worse things happen at sea'. No they don't – take boy-band reunions and party conferences for starters.

So called 'background' music that completely drowns out everything else.

Men over forty wearing baseball hats.

Police referring to men as 'male persons'.

The 'Barmy Army'. I don't dispute that they are indeed true fans but do they have to keep name-checking themselves all the time?

The devaluation of A-level grades. Every year, they keep on getting better, which is plainly ridiculous. The reality is that standards are probably much the same as they were last year and the year before. Which is why they ought to return to the system of the seventies. Then, the assumption was that although exams might vary in difficulty from one year to another, the ability of the students – nationwide – wouldn't. So, every year, the top (say) 10 per cent would be given A grades, the next 15 per cent B grades and so on. It wasn't perfect – and it probably discriminated against marginal candidates – but it did at least have the virtue of consistency.

The words 'Warning – May contain traces of Nuts' on products that obviously contain nuts (e.g. peanut butter).

The words 'Warning – May contain traces of Nuts' on products that couldn't possibly contain nuts (e.g. gooseberry jam) but which might have been made 'in an environment where nuts were present'.

The use of the word 'just' in ads – 'from just £499'.

Self-important TV news foreign correspondents.

Footballers who dive in the penalty area.

'Humorous' birthday cards where the humour relates to the recipient's age/sexual dysfunction/poor memory.

Rolex watch owners. Flash sods.

Celebrity Kabbalah enthusiasts. Especially the ones who wear red string bracelets.

People still using *Fast Show* catchphrases. It doesn't suit them.

Virtual racing and roulette machines in betting shops which makes those shops *de facto* casinos without being subject to the same regulations as casinos.

Employees of large companies who can't help you because 'the computer's down'. No it isn't, is it?

Zany and/or wacky local radio DJs.

Pierced eyebrows. They cause an automatic drop in IQ.

Buses travelling in convoy. I know that I explained why this happens in *Why Girls Can't Throw* but it doesn't make it any less annoying.

Cottaging. Surely no need now, fellas?

Hidden tracks on albums, Always unnecessary.

Bonus tracks on albums. Always awful.

The word 'so' as in 'I am SO not happy'.

ANIMAL RIGHTS

Not to be filmed during sex by TV documentary crews.

Not to be anthropomorphized in Disney movies.

Not to have to smoke untipped cigarettes in laboratories.

Not to be named after soap stars.

Not to be patronized by Rolf Harris.

Not to be used in hamburgers (apart from beef cattle).

Not to appear on *Blue Peter*.

Not to be used in political photo opportunities.

Unworthy celebrities being awarded honorary university doctorates – just so that universities can add a little phony lustre to their degree ceremonies.

Very elderly drivers. They're almost as dangerous as newly qualified teenagers. The number of motorists over 75 has almost trebled in the past quarter century. It's predicted that fatal car crashes involving older drivers will more than double by 2030. Living near Worthing – a.k.a. God's waiting room by the sea – it's not hard to come up with anecdotal evidence: the confused octogenarian who crashed into my wife's parked car without even noticing he'd done so; the almost blind nonagenarian who wrecked the gates at the top of our road simply because he didn't see them. It sounds trivial, comical almost, but that's because it was just a car and not a child, just some gates and not a family. We're told to contact the DVLA if we know an elderly driver who's become a potential menace but no one wants to be a nark and, besides, have you tried to contact the DVLA recently? Understandably, no individual wants to be the one who calls time on an elderly person's liberty. Even the police don't want to know. When my late stepmother discovered that her stepmother (come on, keep up) was still driving despite being almost blind, she thought she'd mention it to the woman's next-door neighbour, who just happened to be a very senior policeman. Was he grateful to be told? No, he was not: in fact, he accused my stepmother of placing him in an awkward position. But who am I to criticize? I used to play bridge with a wonderful old lady who still drove even though she

could barely see the cards, let alone pedestrians. I suggested she stopped, but she said she only drove once a week and then only during the day. So I did nothing. Fortunately, she hung up her keys before she did any damage, but if she'd had an accident, there's no doubt in my mind that I would have borne some responsibility, if only moral. The trouble with the system is that almost all elderly motorists regulate themselves and stop driving when they're ready to but not everyone's judgement is so fine, especially as they get older. Ostensibly, the elderly are subject to annual medical examinations, but these seem to consist of GPs asking: 'You still OK to drive?' and accepting an affirmative answer as proof of competence. Still, it's hard to blame the doctor who shies away from depriving a person of what is probably their last vestige of independence. Ultimately, like so many other aspects of road use, it's a matter of social utility: a balance between reward and risk. Just as we want the emergency services to get where they have to go as quickly as possible without killing anyone along the way, so too do we want elderly people to be independently mobile for as long as possible but without prejudicing the safety of other road users. As it stands at the moment, the balance is too far skewed in favour of the rights of elderly drivers.

Needless background drumming during radio travel announcements.

Doughnuts that ooze out their jam on the wrong side when you bite into them.

People who use finger signs to denote quotation marks.

Politicians claiming that their ambition is 'to make a difference'.

Slappers who run to the papers to sell their stories as soon as they've shagged a footballer or politician. At least prostitutes have the honesty to demand money up front. Worse – much worse – are their 'agents' who get the newspaper deals for them. Sometimes it's hard to distinguish between the sewer and the sewage.

People claiming to be 'happy bunnies'.

'Talking' or musical birthday cards that never shut up.

Other people's children constantly opening such cards in the shop. Even worse in combined newsagent's/post offices with long queues.

Male grooming. Oh *please...*

TV commercials for constipation.

Newspaper reporters showing how easy it is to breach security at airports.

People who say 'Tell me about it...' when you just have.

Blackberry owners who can't stop talking about how much they love their Blackberrys.

Wine connoisseurs. Sniff, twirl, peer, sniff, sip, gargle, spit. Now sod off.

The fetid air on aeroplanes. Back in the bad old days when passengers were allowed to smoke, the airlines were forced to pump more air into the cabins, if only because we could see how awful the air was. Now there's no smoking, the airlines save money by restricting the air supply. Which is why we come off flights feeling like shit.

American TV commercials for hair products aired on British TV.

Travel agents charging more in their shops than they do online.

The expression 'early doors' – as in: 'he'll want to get a goal early doors', or 'I'm off home early doors tonight.'

Old men in sports cars. Just accept that you couldn't afford them when you'd have looked good driving them and settle for something appropriate.

Being expected to tip people – like hotel doormen – who provide no (extra) service whatsoever.

People who wear sunglasses on their heads. Especially annoying if they're in television studios.

Non-Americans who habitually put a 'man' at the end of their sentences.

Scottish Nationalists bleating about independence while enjoying huge subsidies from the rest of us.

All right then. Here's a Scottish Bill of Rights.

ARTICLE 1. All men are created equal and shall respond to the name 'Jimmy' – especially in Glasgow on a Saturday night at closing time.

ARTICLE 2. Only Scottish people (aye an' Sassenachs acting in Bill Forsyth films) will be allowed to use such vernacular expressions as 'hoots mon', 'och aye the noo' and 'wee' and, even then, only whilst in Scotland. In particular we will be keeping an eye on Billy Connolly, Lulu, John Sessions and Tom Conti (though we dinnae ken whit sort o' Scottish name *that* is) an' ithers who act and talk as though bluidy Maidenhead an' Hampstead huv Lothian postcodes.

ARTICLE 3. Scottish children will study a properly Scottish curriculum concentrating on our ain folk like Rabbie Burns, Robert The Bruce, Sean Connery, Slim Jim and Andy Stewart.

ARTICLE 4. Freedom of speech and expression (though see Article 2) is guaranteed to all Scotsmen (the lassies will keep silent). No Scotsman shall be deprived of life, liberty or property nor shall he be obliged to answer any question except 'Who yae gawking at?'

ARTICLE 5. All political parties shall have the right to organize and to stand for election through the due process. However, we the people will no' guarantee the safety of bluidy Conservatives eejits – especially as they don't have any bluidy MPs.

ARTICLE 6. Anyone calling themselves a Scotsman will be obliged to talk like one and to behave like one. The correct answer to 'Will ye no huv a wee dram wi' me?' is 'Aye' and not 'Oh, gosh, I'll have a mineral water, I suppose'.

ARTICLE 7. Although Scotland will be a free country, the people will NOT be allowed to bear arms, except in two instances: i) if attending Old Firm games; ii) if the bluidy English cross the border steamin' oot o' the'r heeds.

ARTICLE 8. Scottish people have the right to be taxed fairly. Although we will be full members of the EU (oor farmers huv nae problem in doon nae wuk) we will no' accept any taxes on whisky – unless the ithers want us to tax their bluidy Perrier water.

ARTICLE 9. The only King that we the Scottish people are prepared to acknowledge is Denis Law and we dinnae gi'e a stuff for the Royal Family. Aye, though but that Princess Anne lassie will always be welcome at Murrayfield.

ARTICLE 10. The oil is bluidy ours.

Footballers' agents. I think we could live without them, don't you?

Taking a day off sick – and then becoming genuinely ill the next day.

People who start their sentences with 'I'm not being funny but…'

Restaurants that add an automatic 15 per cent service charge to the bill. Inevitably provide worse service than restaurants that leave it to our discretion.

People who want to ban films or books they haven't even seen or read. Hand-wringing liberals are just as bad as Bible-bashing conservatives when it comes to this.

Any old model being called a supermodel.

Rock stars' lack of graciousness at awards ceremonies. If they're going to bother turning up they might as well behave themselves.

Jodie Marsh. Makes Jordan look classy.

April Fools' Day pranks. Just like New Year's Eve (qv) brings out the amateur drinkers, April the first encourages dullards to become japesters – with depressing consequences.

MPs waving their order papers and shouting 'hear hear' rather than clapping like normal human beings.

Naomi Campbell. Your life really isn't that awful, pet. So please stop being so angry.

Televangelists. Not so much a problem here as in the States but best hated just in case.

Cockneys. Saying 'we was' instead of 'we were' isn't a dialect, it's just plain wrong.

Celebrities who have novels ghost-written for them. How gullible can the public be? Obviously very.

People with bad breath who insist on sharing it with you. Please feel free not to.

Ultra-modern jazz. Alarmingly atonal. Basically, it's just any number of men all playing different tunes.

The expression 'available in all good bookshops' used in ads for books. So what precisely *is* the definition of a good bookshop? Ah, yes, I thought so. It is in fact any bookshop that happens to stock the book in question. How circularly annoying is that?

Champagne socialists. Let them drink ale.

Bob Geldof's publicity-seeking daughters. I guess with those ridiculous names, it's only to be expected.

Grown men who have to have the latest PlayStation or X-Box model. It's a case of arrested development. In the unlikely event that they have them, pity the girlfriends.

Offal. Awful.

Professional motivators. Those who can do, those who can't teach. Those who can't teach, motivate.

Sports commentators who don't know when to shut up.

Carla Lane moaning about how she can't sell her sitcoms any more. With *Bread*, *The Liver Birds* and *Butterflies* on your CV, I reckon you should be thanking your lucky stars for the run you've already had, love.

Golfing comedians.

Non-Scots celebrating Burns Night. It's even worse if you find yourself at the home of such a person and they feed you haggis. As the clerihew goes, 'One often yearns/For the land of Burns/The only snag is/The haggis.'

Cinema ushers/usherettes. Whatever happened to them? There's never any shortage of miserable spotty minimum-wage munchkins to tear our tickets but none of them ever seems inclined to show us to our seats. Perhaps their torches have been confiscated as potentially lethal weapons.

Travel bores. Yes, I really want to hear all about your trip to Kathmandu. No, honestly. It's just that I concentrate so much better when I shut my eyes.

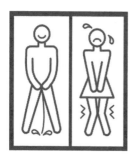

Separate toilets. Why? How stupid is it for a woman to queue for a toilet in a restaurant when the men's toilet is free – and vice-versa? Always provided, of course, that the men's toilet doesn't have a urinal.

Tony Parsons. Pleased with himself or what?

The racket that is estate agency. In the past ten years, house-price inflation has been running at approximately six times the rate of ordinary inflation, but estate agents are still charging an average 2 per cent commission for their services. It would not, they contend, be in the interests of the client to charge a flat rate. Unless we're on commission, they say, how could we be trusted to 'achieve' the highest price? In other words, trust us because we can't be trusted. The theoretical advantage of the commission structure is that the more money you get, the more money they get. However, in practice there isn't that much incentive for them to go the extra yard: they would rather make a quick sale at 95 per cent of the value of your property than work really hard for the 5 per cent that might make all the difference to you.

So here's a tip. Let's say you want to sell your home for £400,000. Tell the agent that instead of giving him 2 per cent of the total (£8,000), he can have 1 per cent on the first £320,000 (that's £3,200), 5 per cent on the next £60,000 (£3,000) and 9 per cent on anything between £380,000 and £400,000. This comes to £8,000. However, it means that instead of persuading you to sell it to the first person who makes you an offer above £380,000, the agent's got a real incentive to sell it at the highest possible price. My last two homes were sold by agents operating on just such a basis and, in both cases, the houses went for the optimistic asking price and the agents ended up with more commission than they would have got on a flat 2 per cent. When it comes to looking after their own interests, you can always trust estate agents.

Dame Shirley Bassey's voice. Could replace Trident.

People – inevitably introspective girls who are having a rotten time at university – who go on about what a genius Sylvia Plath was. She wasn't. So leave your bedsit, go to the union bar and stop feeling so sorry for yourself.

Rory Bremner. I'm old enough to remember when the guy was funny – you know, back in the days before he climbed into his pulpit.

Cereal boxes and packets that are meant to be recloseable but aren't. It just forces you to eat the cereal every day until it's finished. Perhaps that's the point?

People who pronounce 'to' as 'ter'.

People who start their sentences with 'Well, with respect...' and then go on to show none at all.

Local radio DJs constantly name-checking themselves.

Newspaper and magazine articles agonizing over Kate Moss's future. What Should Kate Do Next? I dunno – disappear?

People confusing the words 'your' and 'you're'.

Footballers' WAGs. Anonymity beckons.

Agents who are more famous than their clients.

People talking about their sex lives. Unless they're *really* bizarre and/or unsatisfactory.

Anne Robinson. I don't think she's pretending to be horrible on *The Weakest Link*.

Great actors who go over the top and then proceed to chew up the scenery in every film they make. Think Robert Duvall, Al Pacino, Robert De Niro.

Obsessively secretive celebrities. A simple statement will do.

Daft public-health initiatives – like the state paying for overweight people to join gyms. Why should this fatty pay for another fatty to lose weight? If the government really cared about the nation's health, it would make private health insurance tax deductible.

Marilyn Manson. Strange, very strange.

Spam emails from online casinos offering 300 per cent bonuses. They're not altruists, you know.

People who ask, 'What's the sound of one hand clapping?' In a perfect world, it would be the same sound as the smack on the face of the idiot who asked the question.

American films which use a white person being friendly to a black person as shorthand for the former being a decent person.

Being told by the EU to change the names of Waterloo and Trafalgar Square because they're upsetting for the French. All right then, how about Vichy and Collaborators' Square?

Minor female celebrities who are forced to do promotions for companies making products to combat hair loss.

People who are nostalgic for the Black & White Minstrels. They were horrible even in their heyday.

Terry Gilliam films since *Brazil*. The box office doesn't lie.

Writers whose book jacket photographs don't do them justice. Or, rather, do them too much justice so that when you meet them you get a fright.

Damien Hirst.

People getting offended by Damien Hirst.

'It girls'. What was the point of getting rid of one group of socialite parasites – i.e. debutantes – if they were just going to be replaced with another?

Van Morrison. The voice of an angel, but not the manners. I speak from a bitter experience.

Straight men who lisp.

Comedy double acts with – effectively – two straight men.

Jim Carrey in manic mode.

Edwina Currie. Doesn't get any lovelier as the years pass.

Companies that keep you hanging on the telephone while telling you your call is important to them.

The upgrading of titles that sees a baker becoming a baking operative and a solicitor's clerk becoming a legal executive. Soon it'll be like the States where every executive's a vice-president.

The Germans trying to get our armed forces to come under the direct control of the EU. A German minister has even been quoted as describing the establishment of a single European army as 'the visionary goal of German policy'. You bet. But then, for the Germans, that has always been the whole point of the EU: to achieve through diplomacy what they couldn't achieve through war.

Sycophantic TV interviews of actors and writers.

Houses with security lights that come on whenever anyone walks by.

The paradox that as cars are built to travel faster so the roads become more congested. Frustrating.

AGGRAVATION

Football managers bickering with one another.

Hugh Laurie. Take the Prozac and stop being so bleeding miserable, you wealthy multi-talented depressive.

Quentin Tarantino. Guy makes *Reservoir Dogs*, which was breathtakingly brilliant. Then he follows that up with *Pulp Fiction*, a film so wonderful that you sat there resenting the fact that you would never again see it for the first time. His 'difficult third film' – *Jackie Brown* – was interesting and underrated. Since then? Absolute bollocks; total shite. Is QT – like Orson Welles before him – doomed to live his career in reverse?

People who get embarrassed by strangers' bad behaviour in public – this is a peculiarly English condition.

The constant musical stings on makeover/property TV programmes.

Old Etonians. So you went to a good school. Well, aren't you lucky? Worse though are the ones who refer to Eton as 'school' – as in, 'Was he at school?'

Everything on the internet being priced in dollars, especially gambling sites.

Celebrities being made county high sheriffs or deputy lieutenants. There must be more deserving people, surely?

Women saying, 'It's a girl thing.'

Men saying, 'It's a boy thing.'

Irritating, in-the-way uncle with camcorder at weddings. It's awful: there you are having a good old gossip with one of the few members of your extended family you can actually stand when bloody-in-the-way uncle hoves into view with camcorder – telling you to smile and just catching your perfectly innocent comment about the bride looking like a East End whore on her holidays.

Pub quiz teams who win every week. In practice, they are going to contain a high proportion of men who still live with their mothers. In fact, men over the age of thirty who still live with their mothers should be banned from participating in quiz teams.

Queuing in a post office that has eight customer positions of which only three are open.

Supermarket trolleys with all four wheels going in different directions.

Meaningless (and too loud) background music during otherwise interesting TV documentaries.

Tradesmen saying it's cheaper to pay cash and then charging an exorbitant amount. Without, of course, any guarantees.

Any celebrity who describes him or herself as a 'personality'.

People on diets who criticize what the rest of us eat. OK, Ms/Mr Wonderful, so you're not eating biscuits/crisps/cheese/sweets/chocolates/bread/meat/ice cream or, indeed ANYTHING, at the moment. And that's because? Oh, of course, *because you've done nothing but eat biscuits/crisps/cheese/sweets/chocolates/bread/meat/ice cream/EVERYTHING ever since you first learned to cram food into your fat gob.* Well, bad luck, Billy/Bessie Bunter, but I will NOT be lectured to by you just because you've already eaten all your sweets and, judging by the size of you, everyone else's too. As Orson Welles – no thinso he – so wisely said: 'Gluttony is not a secret vice.' Instead of lecturing me, my friend, why not waddle off and have that tattooed on your soon-to-be-stapled stomach.

Pierced navels on display.

Glottal stops.

Double-yellow lines where single-yellow lines would suffice.

Celebrities who have to have a film crew in tow when they take time off from their careers to try something different.

TV news presenters' phony chat between links.

People – fans, writers, documentary makers – who are still feeding off Marilyn Monroe. The necrophiliacs.

The attitude of (scruffy) record-shop staff.

People who put their own coats on seats on busy trains to look as if they're taken. We've all done it but that doesn't stop it from being a very bad thing to do. Just as bad are the people who choose to sit right next to us on otherwise empty trains.

People imitating Catherine Tate. 'Am I bovvered?' YES.

St Valentine's Day. An opportunity to pay over the odds for a bunch of flowers and to have a row in a crowded restaurant with our loved ones.

Newspaper job ads that 'particularly welcome applications from women, people from the ethnic minority communities and the disabled', where the jobs eventually go to white, able-bodied, middle-aged men. Chairman of the BBC is as good an example as any.

People who use bigger words where smaller ones would do. The vaginas.

The way Gordon Brown opens his mouth like a fish while he pauses for breath when he's speaking.

Men with comb-over hairstyles. They're only fooling themselves.

Twinned towns. I can see why local councillors like having their towns 'twinned' with towns in France and Germany – free or facilitated quasi-state visits. But what's in it for us – you know, the ratepayers who end up paying for it all.

People who believe everything they think.

Radio DJs who cut off records before the end.

TV programmes about cosmetic surgery.

Celebrity exercise videos. Is no aspect of life free from celebrities? What next, Celebrity Russian Roulette? Now *that's* an idea ...

Private security guards who assume greater powers than the police.

British people calling their gardens 'yards' and their flats 'apartments'.

Deliberately ripped jeans.

Text-message speak used anywhere other than in texting.

Other people's bonfires. Applies double on a Sunday.

People who use circles with smiles in them to dot their 'i's. Inexcusable when done by any male or any female over the age of eleven.

Advertising leaflets in newspapers and magazines. Always fall out however carefully you pick up the newspapers or magazines.

Left-wing harridans. Grey hair and a peasant skirt don't make you La Pasionaria.

People who say 'Stop me if you've heard this before' but then don't when you tell them you have.

TV commercials for thrush.

Automated silent calls from companies cold calling.

Fake tribute days invented by the greetings card industry. Happy Ex-Brother-In-Law's Day anyone?

People walking dogs on 200-foot leads.

The expression 'You're joking me'.

'HELL IS PAVED WITH GOOD SAMARITANS.'

William M. Holden

aren, then don't be spelling it Keren
aron or any other way that will cau
e rest of us problems. David Blaine. H
dicrous stunts are more masochis
an magic. People call him the ne
oudini. Well he's not. The point abo
oudini is that he didn't hang around
oxes for forty-four days at a time:
scaped from the   Sunday red-to
bloid new   front   ge storie
ngle man sl   w   le woman
e first date.   him like much
stor   me   isn't. Also ho
n there   appro   h
otba   g with p   ut
d the   g t   in the mornin
After he d   d h   n't wa
know me   e point?
ean, you   umbers
ectricians to   hen they'
one whatever you   them to d
you? So why sh   ts be treate
y differently   ppy G
otherers who s   gs acco
anied by so   ted
guitar. Th   e   ristiani
the hym   Re   and then t
evil really   e all   best tune
xaggeratedly p   ted sho   outside
e circus). People who keep saying 'ye
how what I m n' at the end of the
ntences. Anne a Rice. Truly irritatin
d nakedly ambitious all those yea
go.   Keeps   threatening   to   make
omeback. People falling for those sca
nails from Nigeria. No they haven't

EXASPERATION

David Cameron's attempts to pass himself off as a good bloke to *Guardian* and *Independent* readers who won't vote for him anyway.

People who turn out to be not as nice as the actors or actresses who portray them – e.g. Charles Lindbergh (James Stewart), Maria Von Trapp (Julie Andrews).

Feisty American actresses who come out as lesbians.

Johnny Rotten/Lydon. Tosser then; tosser now.

White Rastafarians. About as sensible as black white supremacists.

The Oxford v. Cambridge Boat Race, or the University Boat Race as they arrogantly call it. I only ever watch it in the hope of a double sinking. Why isn't it open to other universities? It's like the FA Cup final always being between Chelsea and Manchester United. Which of course it is.

Dirty footballers who are lionized by 'lads'. Not big and not clever. Like so many of the culprits themselves.

Sweet, fruity alcoholic drinks. When it comes to their consumption, our girls – or perhaps I should say our 'ladettes' – show a clean pair of white stilettos to the rest of Europe. We're also Number One in Europe for unwanted teenage pregnancies. Connection, perhaps?

Rubik's cube.

Gary Lineker's ads for Walker's Crisps. Game's over, mate.

The freezer. It's like a black hole: any food that goes in there never comes out until you come to dispose of the appliance itself.

'Friends' who can't wait to tell us the awful things that have been said or written about us.

Middle-aged/elderly men – invariably repressed homosexuals with limited vocabularies – who object to the use of the word 'gay' to mean homosexual.

Dog owners who treat their dogs like humans. Invariably treat humans like dogs.

People with absolutely no concept whatever of interior monologue who tell you everything they're thinking.

Sir Andrew Lloyd Webber. Only for his looks and his music and his general manner. His politics are all right.

People complaining they can't afford to live in the villages they grew up in. Move out and move on.

Humourless feminists. Once again, please excuse the tautology. You've won, you've won, now leave us alone. Please.

Stupid spellings of names. If you're a Karen, then don't be spelling it Keren or Caron or any other way that will cause the rest of us problems.

David Blaine. His ludicrous stunts are more masochism than magic. People call him the new Houdini. Well he's not. The point about Houdini is that he didn't hang around in boxes for forty-four days at a time: he escaped from them.

Sunday red-top tabloid newspaper front-page stories. Single man sleeps with single woman on the first date. Doesn't seem like much of a story to me. And so it isn't. Also, how can these rags heap moral opprobrium on footballers for sleeping with prostitutes and then kicking them out in the morning ('After he'd had his way, he didn't want to know me'). Er, isn't that the point? I mean, you don't invite plumbers or electricians to move in when they've done whatever you've paid them to do, do you? So why should tarts be treated any differently?

Happy Clappy God botherers who sing modern songs accompanied by someone not very talented on a guitar. The best thing about Christianity is the hymns. Remove them and then the devil really does have all the best tunes.

WHAT BANKS SAY ...

And What They Really Mean

'Banking with all the latest technology.'
(It still takes a week to send a chequebook.)

'We're your local bank.'
(With a call centre in Calcutta.)

'We'll help you with every aspect of your finances.'
(Yup, we're the kings of cold calling.)

'There is no finer bank.'
(That's because we're all the same.)

'We offer the best interest rates.'
(The highest for borrowers; the lowest for savers.)

'We respond quickly to your needs.'
(Three months' bank charges the second you go overdrawn.)

'All of our university branches have student advisors.'
(Who've been instructed to say 'You can't have an overdraft, mate' instead of 'You can't have an overdraft, sir'.)

'We understand money.'
(That's why we charge you £25 for every letter we send you.)

Exaggeratedly pointed shoes (outside of the circus).

People who keep saying 'you know what I mean?' at the end of their sentences.

Anneka Rice. Truly irritating and nakedly ambitious all those years ago. Keeps threatening to make a comeback.

People falling for those scam emails from Nigeria. No they haven't got several million in a bank and no they won't give you 20 per cent of it if you help them, you sad, deluded puppy.

Bruce Forsyth's catchphrases. And tributes to Bruce Forsyth.

People asking whether it's 'Hot enough for you?' whenever the sun comes out.

French people refusing to speak English. We know they do when our backs are turned.

Mechanics tutting under their breath when our cars are having their MOTs.

People chewing gum with their mouths open.

The police 'interviewing' people for saying or doing politically incorrect things – like selling golliwogs.

Polite notices – meant to look like 'police' notices.

Empty supermarket shelves marked 'Best Bargains'.

The misuse of the word 'decimated' to mean a complete annihilation when in fact it means the removal of one in ten.

Hugh Fearnley-Whittingstall. Placenta-cooking tosser.

Two TV newsreaders when one would do.

British people employing the Australian inflection so that every sentence sounds like it's a question. Doubly worse when done by a girl who's been to Sydney for a week and claims that she can't help it – or, rather, that she can't help _it_.

People who say, 'That's for me to know and you to find out.'

That woman on _Dragon's Den_. Ooh dear, there's an ugly tree somewhere with a lot of branches missing.

Middle-aged women who do the abandoned-hands-in-the-air-would-be-hippy-chick dance at rock festivals. Get back to your Agas.

People who say 'I'm loving it' or, worse, 'I'm lovin' it'. I'm hatin' it.

Cinema ads warning us about pirate videos. Time was when cinemagoers were 'patrons'; now we're treated like potential delinquents.

School inset days. Aren't the school holidays long enough for teachers?

Media studies degrees. I know that Labour wants half of all 18-year-olds to go on to further education but this inevitably leads to second-rate universities churning out unemployable media studies graduates by the thousand. The knock-on effect of this is that these graduates have to be prepared to work for nothing just to have the chance of a job in a ludicrously overcrowded field. Poor sods.

Once funny American comics who become unfunny actors. Think Chevy Chase, Steve Martin, Eddie Murphy.

Satanists. Silly boys.

P. Diddy/Puff Daddy/Sean Combs. Make your mind up, son.

Newspaper fashionistas. Almost all ugly old harridans.

Being told 'what's hot and what's not!' by fashionistas who made it up in the back of the taxi on their way into the office.

The veneration of Joe Orton. He was young! He was gay! He was murdered! So what? He was only a mediocre playwright.

Writers who use their initials instead of their first names. I've got a truly stupid first name and I don't.

Finance and insurance companies that appropriate what you might call 'heritage' names like Admiral or Hastings or Churchill to make themselves sound ultra-dependable.

Nigella Lawson. Mrs Cholmondley-Warner shows you how to eat. I've met her a few times and she's always looked at me as though I had a bogey hanging out of one of my nostrils. Who knows? Maybe, I did – once. But surely not *every* time.

People who claim to have read *A Brief History of Time*. No, they didn't.

Gonzo American porn films involving double anal entry. Not very clever. Even if the 'actress' is consenting, it's still wrong.

Politicians apologizing for bad things that happened in history for which they weren't responsible, e.g. slavery, but refusing to apologize for the bad things for which they were responsible.

Prince Albert rings. Why? I'm crossing my legs just at the thought.

Tie-less Tory MPs. It's the ties that bind.

Police distributing leaflets 'naming and shaming' persistent offenders. The trouble with scum though is that no matter how much you name them, you'll never shame them.

Minor celebrities who turn out to be surprisingly pleasant when you meet them and even suggest going out for lunch but who, when you ask them for their phone number (to arrange lunch), give you their agent's number.

Russian gangsters in Russia. I was in Russia recently and I was struck by how much of a hold organized crime has on everyday life. The country's gone from communism to gangsterism without a second's pause for capitalism. We may not always like our system but as Churchill said, 'Democracy is the worst form of government except for all the others that have been tried.' The Russians deserve nothing less.

Pete Burns. Dead Or Alive, eh? I know which I'd prefer.

Hip-hop. Not to forget hip-hoppers.

Michael Jackson. Obviously none of us *knows* what went on at Michael Jackson's Neverland ranch but what I don't get is how parents allowed their children to go over there for 'sleepovers' in the 'secret room'. Yes, I know that parents have to use judgement but in situations like this parents aren't judges – they're advocates for their children. If there's *any* doubt then their instinct must be to protect their children and give them, rather than Jackson, the benefit of it.

Virgin. How can (what is basically) the same company offer such luxury in its planes and yet such misery on its trains?

Sir Salman Rushdie. Not much of a fatwah, was it?

The expression 'I feel your pain'. No you don't – so stop taking the piss.

Celebrities – like Carol Vorderman – advertising loan products.

Celebrities – like Carol Vorderman – promoting diets.

Cinemagoers who think that the words please switch off your mobile phone' don't apply to them.

Being told to 'cheer up, it may never happen'. It just did – thanks to them.

Shop assistants who say 'There you go' when handing over goods. Don't you patronize me, you minimum-wage slave.

Cheap, flimsy carrier bags with 'handles' that are strong enough to cut right through our fingers but that break as soon as we put anything inside the bags. Very strange.

EXASPERATION

Marks & Spencer not having loos in all their stores.

Woody Allen films of the past fifteen years. He's lost his mojo.

Miracle diets. The only miracle is that anyone falls for them.

Mobile phone ringtones that sound nothing like the songs they're supposed to be.

Mobile phone ringtones that sound just like the songs they're supposed to be.

People nagging me to go on Fun Runs. Never was there a greater oxymoron than the expression 'fun run'.

Vanessa Redgrave. Not because she's a communist – well, not just – but because she's really, *really* scary...

Trailers that give away half the story.

Children In Need. No 'need' justifies this smug-fest.

Newsreaders pronouncing 'Glasgow' in a Glaswegian accent when they don't pronounce 'Birmingham' in a Brummie accent.

97

The honours system. As Mark Twain said, 'It is better to deserve honours and not have them than to have them and not deserve them.'

Some People Who *Really* Deserve Honours:

Prince Harry's bodyguard.

Liz Taylor's divorce lawyer.

Jodie Marsh's press agent.

Anne Robinson's plastic surgeon.

Dawn French's furniture upholsterer.

Jade Goody's agent.

Some People Who Really *Don't* Deserve Honours:

Victoria Beckham's singing tutor.

Camilla Parker Bowles's couturier.

Robbie Coltrane's personal trainer.

Margaret Beckett's beautician.

Harry Hill's hairdresser.

Eddie Izzard's dressmaker.

The word 'attitude' used to describe rudeness and arrogance. Just tell it like it is.

TV weather presenters trying to become TV personalities. Just give us the facts, Jack.

Men wearing earrings, unless they're gypsies or pirates.

The use of the word 'London' in London Gatwick (Sussex), London Stansted (Essex) and London Luton (Bedfordshire). Can you imagine what a foreigner arriving in London Luton feels like when he realizes just how far he is from Piccadilly Circus? The worst example, however, isn't an airport but a cruise terminal. Harwich is eighty miles from the centre of London but that doesn't stop cruise operators calling it London (Harwich) or Harwich (London). Still, you've got to laugh.

Footballers feigning injury during a match – i.e. cheating on their fellow professionals.

Call-centre staff with incomprehensible accents. Here or overseas.

Incredibly patronizing female children's TV presenters.

The expression 'It's political correctness gone mad'.

Ludicrously overpaid BBC presenters who then go on to do voiceovers for Tesco (I know, every little helps…).

Sad sacks who 'buy' mail-order brides from Thailand, the Philippines or Russia.

People – especially celebrities – who treat their friends like sidekicks. No one needs an entourage.

Posh people pontificating in posh accents at football matches.

People who invoke Nazi Germany in arguments. 'I think we should ban foxhunting.' 'Oh do you? Well that's what they did in Nazi Germany.' And your point is?

Men who stand right next to you in public urinals when there's plenty of space elsewhere.

Almost anything Madonna does – but especially Kabbalah.

The expression 'You do the math'.

Drivers going past speed cameras at 12 mph just to be on the safe side. You don't rack up brownie points, you know.

Blatant product placement in films. Destroys the film's integrity.

People who join MENSA. Sad, desperately sad. Well, consider the following members: Sir Clive Sinclair, Sir Jimmy Savile, Carol Vorderman, Garry Bushell, Carol Smillie, Jamie Theakston. Far better to be measured at above MENSA entry level and then not join – like John Thomson, Caroline Aherne, Bill Clinton, James Woods and Jessica Simpson.

Famous people who bang on about their bloody dyslexia.

QUESTIONS OF ETIQUETTE POSED BY BLOODY CALL WAITING

If you phone someone and get Call Waiting, is it more polite to hang up or stay on?

If you do hang up, are you obliged to let that person know later that it was you they heard on their Call Waiting?

Should the person who has the Call Waiting carry on with the first conversation?

If he/she does, should he/she ask the second caller to wait?

If he/she does ask the caller to wait and then keep them waiting a long time, should he/she offer to pay for that caller's call?

If the person who has Call Waiting decides to get rid of the first caller, should the first caller ever bother to phone him/her again?

If they do, should they put the phone down immediately if they get Call Waiting?

If they wait, should they insist to the person who has the Call Waiting that, on the basis of historical precedent, they are obliged to take this, the second call?

If the person who has the Call Waiting doesn't agree, should the caller put the phone down and come round to give him/her a piece of his/her mind?

The expression 'friendly fire'. Almost as bad is 'blue on blue', which sounds like a porn film.

Websites that inhibit your back button so that you can't get back to where you were. Particularly annoying on porn sites, which is where, of course, it mostly happens.

Brazilian waxing. What kind of man finds a bald binky sexy? And why would any woman want to hook up with the sort of man who finds a bald binky sexy?

The word 'genius' used to describe a very ordinary artiste.

The cost of rail travel. With all the fares on offer, you'd think that *one* of them would be acceptable.

Hot dogs and burgers at football matches. Verrucas, testicles, toenails in a bun. Yummy.

The Notting Hill Set. Tossers.

The Primrose Hill Set. Useless tossers.

People who have cosmetic surgery for, er, purely cosmetic reasons.

Modern films that are at least an hour longer than they need to be. It's as if the producers, having paid millions to get their stars, are determined to get their money's worth. Rule of thumb: no thriller should ever be longer than two hours and no comedy should last longer than a hundred minutes.

People who refer to themselves in the third person. Very common among rock stars and boxers. And third-world despots.

Tiny dogs carried by female stars as fashion accessories.

People who say 'fact' at the end of their sentences as though saying that automatically proves them right.

People still saying, 'You ARE the weakest link.'

The word 'ONLY!', used in any form of advertising.

Weather forecasters who tell us to drive carefully in bad weather (we're not stupid).

Motorists who drive recklessly in bad weather (they, alas, *are* stupid).

Shaven-headed men with vicious dogs in parks.

People who use supermarket car parks as racetracks.

Companies giving themselves pseudo-Latin names in an attempt to project gravity and probity.

Traffic lights that are red for ninety seconds and green for just ten.

Buying things we never use.

Some of the Things You Wish You Hadn't Bought:

The breadmaking machine (never been taken out of the box).

The juicer (used once but never cleaned).

The exercise bicycle (currently used as a clothes horse).

The electronic bathroom scales that measure your Body Mass Index (never set up).

The fish cookbook (unopened).

The indoor putting machine (still awaiting batteries).

The set of encyclopedias (untouched because they've been superseded by Google).

The sit-up machine (poorly assembled – by you – and so it looks OK but doesn't work).

The weather-forecasting kit (buried beneath your shoes).

Ad breaks five minutes into TV programmes.

Radio DJs' sidekicks. Unnecessary. Just spin the platters that matter.

Lunchtime queues at the bank. Kind of predictable, no, on both parts?

Extravagant thanks from TV newsreaders to colleagues (e.g. weather presenters).

Bob Geldof singing 'I Don't Like Mondays' – i.e. a medley of his hit – at charity concerts. Let someone else have a chance, Bob.

Unsatisfying standard replies from big companies to our genuine complaints.

Non-soldiers wearing 'combat gear'.

Trailers for TV programmes due to start in two minutes.

The use of the word 'brave' to describe a celebrity's endurance of self-inflicted wounds (i.e. drug addiction).

Broadcasters cutting to commercials every time a wicket is taken during satellite coverage of Test matches. Don't they derive enough money from our subscriptions, the greedy bastards?

Inflated RRPs in newspaper ads so that retailers can show us the huge 'saving' they're giving us. We're not stupid, you know. Well, not all of us.

People who still think it's funny to do Austin Powers impersonations. Two words: be have.

Smug, self-righteous, anti-smoking fanatics.

The words 'he was stood' or 'he was sat' instead of 'standing' and 'sitting'.

TV ads for cat food.

The pimp roll. Not very appealing but given that they're probably carrying a Stanley knife, who's going to tell them?

Cyclists wearing iPods. Can't hear/won't hear. Won't live.

Tourists who enter crowded trains or lifts wearing backpacks almost as big as themselves. The rule is: the bigger the backpack, the less they're contributing to our economy. So piss off back to Scandinavia, Sven, but feel free to leave your cute girlfriend here.

People who persist in doing Ali G impressions. It wasn't even that funny when Sacha Baron Cohen did them.

Tracey Emin's 'art'. I saw her Unmade Bed at the Saatchi Gallery and the (sick) joke is that there was a curator on hand to make sure that no one tried to change it. What difference would it have made?

Internet angst: the very real fear that we might not have found the rock-bottom price for a flight/book/ticket we bought on the net.

Sententious newspaper columnists who write as if the hand of history were lying heavily on their shoulders. It's only tomorrow's fish and chip wrapping.

Newspaper Columnist Speak:

'I was reading in the paper the other day.' (Don't think I don't do any research.)

'As any mother will tell you.' (Or, indeed, the children's nanny.)

'I was talking to this taxi-driver.' (I still have contact with working people.)

'Something must be done.' (But not, of course, by me.)

'I'm all for freedom of speech …' (Don't be silly.)

'He should try working for a living.' (Just look at me: five three-hour lunches a week and I still manage to write a thousand words.)

'What really concerns me…' (… and my editor and proprietor.)

'It makes you think, doesn't it?' (Well, it took me an extra five minutes to write the column this week.)

'The solution is simple.' (Regular readers will have guessed as much.)

'It came as no surprise to learn.' (Thank God for hindsight.)

THINGS THAT SEEM TO MAKE OTHER PEOPLE SMILE BUT JUST MAKE ME ANNOYED

'Funny' birthday cards.

Mr Bean.

Practical jokes.

Any programme starring Frank Skinner.

Peanuts.

Charlie Chaplin films.

Ken Dodd's Diddymen.

The work of Spike Milligan.

Fancy-dress costumes worn by the crowd at sports matches.

American teen sitcoms shown here on satellite TV.

Wallace & Gromit.

Sat-navs that make us dependent on them and then go on to abuse our trust by sending us on four-hour journeys to destinations two hours away (I write from experience, you'll understand).

Celebrities who put their names to products they wouldn't ordinarily use. The corporate shills.

British beaches polluted by raw sewage. Not as bad as it was but it's still unacceptable for *any* of our beaches not to attain blue-flag status.

Being pestered in the street by paid 'chuggers' to make standing orders for charities.

Professional Tykes who don't live in Yorkshire. If you love Yorkshire so much, you could always move there, you know. (See also Professional Jocks and Professional Scousers.)

TV chefs trying to persuade us to eat scary cuts of meat like pig's trotters, cow's eyeballs, sheep's udders.

Shops that have year-round sales. They're a con.

Supermarkets that say 'There's no call for it' when you ask them why they no longer stock your favourite food.

Fair Trade products. Does this mean that all the other products we import are unfair trades?

Politicians priding themselves on being 'inclusive'.
Only when it comes to photo opportunities.

Women showing off tattoos.

Shops advertising a discount on the shelf or display
and then charging the full price at the checkout.

The FCUK logo. It's pahtetic.

Knighthoods given to time-serving politicians. The
Tories are the villains when it comes to this.

**TV sports presenters taking the Paralympics seriously. It's
either occupational therapy or a freak show. What it *isn't*
is a proper sporting contest, primarily because the pool
of participants is so small. You can admire them for their
courage and their determination, but as TV sport it's
meaningless.**

Greedy developers building a dozen new houses on a plot barely big enough for two.

**Stupid people in large groups. Fortunately we don't have
lynch mobs any more – well, not really – but that doesn't
stop people from saying and doing scary things in crowds
that they wouldn't dare do individually. Think of football
supporters or a group of self-righteous vigilantes
complaining about paedophiles, or indeed paediatricians.**

Companies that invoke comparisons with NASA or the space programme in TV commercials.

British youngsters behaving like sex-crazed drunken louts in continental resorts.

Newspapers sending reporters to continental resorts to find British youngsters misbehaving themselves.

Incorrectly set temporary traffic lights on quiet country lanes.

Anyone with more than two cats. It's a big tell.

Builders who never come when they say they will.

People who throw litter out of moving cars.

Supermarket shoppers ahead of me in the queue who don't pull out their purses until the total comes up. And then use a credit card to pay for purchases less than £10.

People who are jammed on transmit.

The expression 'loved up' as in 'Demi Moore and Ashton Kutcher are loved up'.

People who grab the comfy chairs in trendy coffee shops and stay there for hours – forcing the rest of us to drink our overpriced coffees on the hard seats. Still, serves us right for going there in the first place. You pay half as much in an ordinary cafe *and* they serve you at your table.

Celebrities who deny having had (very obvious) cosmetic surgery.

People who stare at your worst feature – especially if it's a huge spot – when they talk to you.

Local newsreaders who thank national newsreaders when they (the national newsreaders) obviously can't hear them.

Fat/pregnant girls wearing crop-tops.

People who drive miles to fill up their cars before Budget increases kick in.

Newspapers claiming stories as exclusives when all the other papers are carrying them. Also, newspapers – especially red-top tabloids – putting 'exclusive' over the top of a story that no other paper could be bothered to run.

People sniffing instead of blowing their nose. Why don't men (especially) carry handkerchiefs any more?

Other people's speed camera stories. Yeah, yeah, we know.

Ninety-second pauses when the results are given in reality TV shows.

Seat-belt buzzers in cars. Don't you *dare* tell us what to do.

Waiting in a supermarket queue when a new checkout is opened and people who have been standing behind you end up getting served before you.

TV programmes 'recorded before a live studio audience'. And what other kind of studio audience is there?

Charities that send us free pens in a bid to make us feel obligated to them.

Feeling guilty when we keep the pens that come with charity appeals and throw away the letters.

People who call other people 'muppets'.

TV commercials for wrinkly products (e.g. stairlifts, walk-in baths) featuring people who clearly don't need them.

Unsolicited advice.

Politicians describing suicide/homicide bombers as 'cowardly'. Anyone prepared to give up their lives for their beliefs might justifiably be described as single-minded, mad and fanatical – but never cowardly. Besides, bravery in no way mitigates evil.

Terrible American remakes of classic British movies like *Get Carter* and *The Italian Job*.

The English apologizing for being English. Cecil Rhodes said that to be English was to have 'won first prize in the lottery of life'. He should see us now. We're too supine. We tolerate speed cameras and sewage in the sea. Yet there's still hope. There's an Englishness that transcends our embarrassment and our timidity. It's not the usual outdated stereotypes like pearly kings and queens or Morris dancers or warm beer in pubs. It's also not about being Anglo-Saxon: some of our greatest Englishmen are Gujarati, Sikh, Jewish, Muslim and Hindi, who are only first-generation English. The Englishness I'm thinking of is what we are and what we do. It's tending allotments and doing DIY; it's HP Sauce, marmalade and salad cream; it's having Barbara Windsor as a sex symbol and remembering (if you're over fifty) where you were when Geoff Hurst completed his hat-trick in the World Cup Final; it's planning our lives around the weather forecast without trusting it; it's having more public parks and public libraries than anywhere else; it's Mrs Slocombe's pussy and Blakey saying 'I hate you, Butler'; it's having a different accent from people living twenty miles away; it's scoring at a county cricket match in the rain; it's finding bluebells in April; it's the music of Billy Bragg, Benjamin Britten and Ray Davies and the poetry of Philip Larkin, Stevie Smith and John Betjeman. It's understatement; it's tolerance; it's Englishness. And one of the best things – the very best things – about being English is that we don't have to celebrate St George's Day. Especially when we can whinge about not celebrating it instead.

'I hate you, Butler'

People having their tattoos removed on the NHS. Tattoo parlours should have to pay a special tax that would pay for such treatment.

The use of the word 'organic' when applied to music.

Editors' 'letters' in the front of magazines – especially when accompanied by touched-up photos.

The Liberal Democrats. You used to know where you were with the Liberal Party. It was the None Of The Above party that provided a home for Tories-with-consciences, socialists-with-humanity or just plain liberals. They had beards and wore sandals – and that was just the women. They were led by the thoroughly decent Jo Grimond and the whole of the Parliamentary party could fit comfortably into a single taxi (Cyril Smith hadn't yet taken his seats). Even if you dismissed them as eccentrics you respected their integrity. To poke fun at them was fine but any more was unkind, like shooting fish in a barrel. Times have changed and so, alas, have the Liberals. They've become ambitious. As the two main political parties scrap for the middle ground the Liberals have reinvented themselves as a political force to be diluted according to taste. In the South-west they are conservatives, in Scotland they are big-spending devolutionists, in the cities they are simply Old Labour. They are the political equivalent of litmus paper. If New Labour 's theme song was 'Things Can Only Get Better' (and how hollow that sounds now), the Liberals' is 'Whatever You Want'. But don't listen to me. Let them condemn

themselves. The advice in the official Liberal Party
Guide For Councillors And Campaigners reads: 'In
simple terms, if it's a Labour council you can secure
support from voters who normally vote Tory by being
effectively anti-Labour and similarly in a Tory area
secure Labour votes by being anti-Tory. Be wicked, act
shamelessly, stir endlessly.' The only thing the Liberals
really do stand for is proportional representation – that
electoral fix whereby they become the permanent
fixture in every coalition government.

**British politicians' flakiness when it comes to Gibraltar.
The Spanish have made their wishes clear but then so
have the people of Gibraltar who consistently vote (almost)
unanimously to remain British. It's no use fighting for the
democratic rights of Iraqis if we deny them to Gibraltarians.
Gibraltar's sovereignty is non-negotiable.**

Deckchairs. I can't work 'em out – which makes me feel stupid.

Celebrity single mothers. It sets a bad example.

Being kept on hold when phoning big companies.

**Charity wristbands. All of 'em – even the ones for worth-
while causes – because they're almost always worn by
people to show off their moral superiority.**

The word 'über' used before almost any adjective.

People with facial piercings. Wouldn't it be cheaper – not to say less painful – just to wear a T-shirt saying 'I'M A TOTAL TOSSER'?

People who say 'I was like' instead of 'I said'.

Clothes that are ruined in the wash – even when we've followed the instructions to the letter.

Michael Moore documentaries.

Loos in other people's homes that don't flush properly.

Thin celebrities/Thick celebrities.

Eddie Murphy's voiceovers for animated films. Applies double if he's playing an animal as a street-smart (but lovable) rogue.

The gooey look that female TV news presenters fix on their male co-presenters while the latter are speaking, as if to say: 'Have I ever told you, you're my hero?'

Abandoned supermarket trolleys.

Supermarkets refusing to pick up abandoned super-market trolleys – even when you've phoned them half a dozen times.

People who don't open doors for other people when they've had doors opened for themselves. There might also be a metaphor in there somewhere too.

EXASPERATION

SIGNS THAT THE SCHOOL SUMMER HOLIDAYS HAVE STARTED

Teachers stop moaning about their pay and conditions.

Travel agents put their prices up.

The roads are clear.

Supermarkets reverberate to the sound of a hundred children exclaiming, 'I'm bored!'

There are mass outbreaks of graffiti.

Public swimming pools are even more highly chlorinated than usual.

Your dustbin has been appropriated as a cricket wicket.

Mothers are spotted ticking days off calendars.

There isn't a single non-retractable aerial left standing in the road.

You can't find a local cinema that isn't showing bloody kids' films.

You can't walk fifty yards without being knocked over by a skateboard.

W.H. Smith's puts 'Back to School' signs in their windows.

SIGNS THAT THE SCHOOL SUMMER HOLIDAYS HAVE ENDED

Teachers can be heard moaning about their pay and conditions.

The price of package holidays goes down.

Public swimming pools are once again 100 per cent water.

The roads are blocked.

Mothers are spotted with smiles on their faces.

Your children once again become friends with that ghastly child 'Everybody Else', as in 'Everybody Else has got one'.

Amusement arcades don't bother opening till four o'clock.

W.H. Smith's puts up 'Ideas for Christmas' in their windows.

The Americanism 'hurting' (as in 'you shouldn't have been so cruel to her: she's really hurting').

Big Brother winners being treated as celebrities instead of the freak-show participants they really are.

Dog poo in parks.

Complementary therapists who've done less than three years' training. Basic rule of thumb is that the benefit of any complementary therapy is in inverse proportion to the amount of time it takes to qualify as a therapist. So osteopathy, which takes several years, is incredibly beneficial, while aromatherapy, which takes as long as – ooh – two weeks on a correspondence course, is totally useless.

The expression 'How long's a piece of string?'

The absurd importance attached to what's said on Radio 4's *Today* programme.

Know-nothing youths in call centres being described as 'advisors'.

Waiters/waitresses who don't apologize when something has gone wrong – on the basis that it wasn't their (personal) fault.

Computerized hotel keycards that only work intermittently.

Being offered free balance checks by cashpoint machines that charge us to withdraw money.

The word 'closure' as in 'They're trying to achieve closure on this issue'.

Coca-Cola Zero and Pepsi Max. Unnecessary and confusing in a world that has Diet Coke and Diet Pepsi.

Minor celebrities who check in to the Priory as a career move.

TV commercials for toenail infections. Never pretty.

Men who boast about their vasectomies. The fools.

Women who try to pressurize their menfolk to have vasectomies.

People who join – or, worse, try to join – the mile-high club on anything other than a private plane.

TV newsreaders who say 'I'll see you later' instead of 'You can see me later'.

Tesco's 'every little helps' slogan.

House-buyers who describe themselves as 'cash buyers' when they have in fact got a house to sell.

British tourists abroad wearing Union Jack clothing.

Spoof TV chat shows. Done to death.

Junior salesmen calling themselves 'executives'.

People who say 'Don't give up the day job' to anyone trying their hand at something new.

Vic & Bob – and the people who lionize(d) them. Talk about the Emperor's New Clothes.

People who call Christmas 'Chrimbo'. Happens more than you think.

Parents who get their (tiny) children to record their answering-machine messages for them.

Footballers arguing with referees.

Senior executives of public companies being given huge bonuses even when their companies have performed badly.

Women on hen nights.

People downloading each and every one of their digital holiday photos – the modern equivalent of those dreaded slideshows of yesteryear – for the supposed edification of their guests.

Traffic lights on roundabouts. No need.

Fat people claiming that they've got a slow metabolism or they're big boned. No one came out of Belsen needing to lose weight.

Boy racers in pathetic cars with massive spoilers.

'HELL IS ONESELF:
HELL IS ALONE. THE OTHER
FIGURES IN IT MERELY PROJECTIONS.
THERE IS NOTHING TO ESCAPE FROM
AND NOTHING TO ESCAPE TO.
ONE IS ALWAYS ALONE.'

George Eliot

rofits. In a civilized society, there ...
ome services – like the post – that shou...
e allowed to run on a non-profit basis...
ven at a loss. That's why we call th...
ervices and not businesses. T...
ssumption that the idiots who queue ...
ight for Wimbledon tickets are someh...
EAL tennis fans and are therefore ...
uch more entitled to be there than t...
at cats' who are Pimmsed and dined ...
he corporate hospitality tents. T...
ueuers aren't ... fans; they ...
Wimbledon fans, ... ally loved t...
port – ... opp... occasion...
hey'd go ... al... ten...
ournament... verbial m...
nd his dog ... official atte...
ance. Peo... oth...
eople s... one wo...
or 'em. ... ue on t...
erest prete... ju... they thi...
here's a dr... in i... them. ople w...
ay how m... th... Jam s Joy...
hey're ...ing. ... sa...
bout U... su...
osh.' Eve... his...
Why don... people ...
ead?' Me... ds are as b...
s they're ... Dennis ... ner. Lov...
y the le... ged by th right. Wh...
elf-importan... executiv... t's not...
rown-up job, you know. Engla...
ootball managers. Useless buggers t...
t of them. Except Sir Alf. Mohamed...
ayed. Sometimes in my really da...
oments, the only thing that keeps me...

IRASCIBILITY

Having to reproduce impossible-to-read letters on websites to prove that we're not spammers.

Trade-union leaders who live much more lavishly than their members do.

A society in which criminals' rights trump the rights of their victims. There is a desperate need for greater justice – particularly when it comes to crimes that affect the individual.

Parents who work all hours then say they have QUALITY TIME with their children. Children don't have a concept of 'quality time': they just want to know that Mum and/or Dad are there when *they* (the children) need or want them.

Standing ovations for leaders at party conferences. As guaranteed as the National Anthem at the Last Night of the Proms – and just as stage-managed.

The pressure on the Royal Mail to make profits. In a civilized society, there are some services – like the post – that should be allowed to run on a non-profit basis or even at a loss. That's why we call them services and not businesses.

The assumption that the idiots who queue all night for Wimbledon tickets are somehow REAL tennis fans and are therefore so much more entitled to be there than the 'fat cats' who are Pimmsed and dined in the corporate hospitality tents. The queuers aren't tennis fans: they're Wimbledon fans. If they really loved the sport – as opposed to the occasion – they'd go to all the other British tennis tournaments where the proverbial man and his dog constitute the official attendance.

People who can't abhor other people swearing. There's only one word for 'em.

Celebrities who sue on the merest pretext, just because they think there's a drink in it for them.

People who say how much they love James Joyce. They're lying. As Virginia Woolf said about *Ulysses*: 'Never have I read such tosh.' Even Joyce's wife Nora asked him: 'Why don't you write books people can read?'

Most modern art. Things are as bad as they're painted.

Dennis Skinner. Loved by the left; indulged by the right. Why?

Self-important TV executives. It's not a grown-up job, you know.

England football managers. Useless buggers the lot of them. Except Sir Alf.

Mohamed Al-Fayed. Sometimes in my really dark moments, the only thing that keeps me in this country is the fact that Fayed isn't a British citizen. I love the way that we give ANY Tom, Dick or Ali citizenship at the drop of a hat but there's this geezer who buys Harrods and is a multi-millionaire and whenever he asks, the answer's always the same: NAAAAAHHHHH! God, it makes me proud to be British.

Parents who take their children to the doctor with minor injuries (like a grazed knee).

Very minor celebrities who complain about stalkers. Just be grateful that anyone can be bothered.

People who belittle our ambitions.

Foxhunters who go on about how much they respect foxes. Leave it out.

People who insert a 'de' in their surname in an attempt to sound posh.

Prince Edward. His title alone should be enough to make him interesting. Alas, this drain on the public purse is a charisma-free zone. Still, he is at least good for a laugh. When his wife gave birth to their first kid ('Congratulations, ma'am, you've given birth to a minor royal'), the prince indicated that he would be taking paternity leave. Which begged the thought: as opposed to doing what?

Another thing. Why do fawning commentators refer to him as 'the Prince Edward'? Is there another Prince Edward – a bogus wannabe Prince Edward – doing the rounds?

Men who buy Ferraris in a country with a speed limit of 70mph. And no, city boy, you're not going to be driving it on the autobahn.

Calls for public inquiries when high-profile prisoners like Harold Shipman kill themselves. Although I'm totally opposed to the death penalty, I've no problem whatsoever with murderers such as Shipman – yes, and Brady, Whiting and Huntley – killing themselves. Let them check out any time they like – because they can never leave. If the prison service wants to reproach itself for not preventing suicides, it should instead be looking at young offenders' institutions such as Feltham, which have a terrible suicide record. Except that when it comes to inquiries – public or otherwise – delinquent teenagers don't have quite the same cachet as mass murderers.

**Car owners who use an unusual font for their number plate.
Why would they want to and how come they're allowed to?**

Celebrities who treat autograph-hunting children like
shit. Which is my way of getting back at Warren
Mitchell more than forty years after the event.

**Women who become minor celebrities by dint of being
married to someone famous who then try to remain minor
celebrities even after they divorce their famous husbands.**

Massive bonuses for City boys. I don't object in
principle – just in practice. Pure jealousy, I'm afraid.

British people who own second homes in the UK. Greedy tossers.

Stan Collymore. You don't hit women. Ever. Not even Ulrika.

Dubbed laughter. Or, just as bad, audience laughter
cued and whipped up by the floor manager.

Uri Geller.

Childcare experts. Especially childless ones.

**Jack Straw. The Vicar of Bray is looking down, rubbing his
hands and purring, 'That's my boy.'**

The refusal of state and society to deal with prostitution in a grown-up way. Of all the professions, prostitution is reckoned to be the oldest. The second oldest is, of course, politics, but while prostitutes have often looked after the needs of politicians, there's been precious little reciprocity. The existing legislation is complicated, contradictory and seemingly devised to punish women whose only 'crime' is that they choose to sell their bodies. Here's just one example. If, for their own protection, two prostitutes decide to work from the same address then they are deemed to be operating a brothel. The fact is that in any well-ordered society, there should always be an assumption that what consenting adults do in private is entirely up to them. However, there are in that sentence three key words, 'consenting', 'adults' and 'private' and, currently, all three of them are in jeopardy. Not all prostitutes are consenting. Women looking to escape poverty in Eastern Europe or South America are brought or lured here and are then forced to work as sex slaves. Not all prostitutes are adults. There are many under-age girls – many of them ostensibly 'in care' – working as street prostitutes. According to a report by ECPAT (End Child Prostitution, Pornography and Trafficking), Britain has become the hub of a growing trade in children from overseas. Not all prostitutes work in private. Many of our towns and cities are blighted by street prostitution, which causes understandable offence to residents and provokes real fear in women mistakenly propositioned by men whose brains are in their trousers. That's the way it is. Prostitution is rife. The law says it ought to be otherwise but you

might as well try to legislate against the tide.

Some men choose to pay women for sex; some women choose to provide sex for money. It's their choice. It's not up to the rest of us to be judgemental. All we're entitled to do is ensure that society is protected against the genuinely criminal aspects of prostitution that should provide the entire focus of the Vice Squad's work. Getting rid of the petty laws would go a long way towards getting rid of the coercive pimps and their terrified victims. Prostitution must be legalized and regulated for everyone's sake. 'Working girls' should be allowed to operate from private premises or in licensed brothels but not on the streets. They should be allowed to advertise – though not in telephone boxes. With rights, however, come responsibilities: they should be obliged to have regular health screenings and they should also pay tax on their earnings. As for their clients, kerb crawling should remain an offence. In addition, any man who pays for sex with a girl under 18 should be automatically prosecuted. Once these legitimate concerns have been addressed, the state must back off. Let's face it, it has taken long enough. The effective legalization of prostitution is the last frontier in the sexual revolution that started in the Sixties. You and I might not want any part of it but all the evidence is there to prove that thousands of citizens do. Who are we to criminalize them?

Any newspaper or magazine article beginning 'It is a truth universally acknowledged that an *X* in possession of a *Y* must be in want of a *Z*'.

The Olympics being staged in the UK in 2012. Just what we need: more visitors and more expense. And we won't win any more medals than we usually do.

Monosodium glutamate in Chinese restaurants. Always screws up my head and stomach for days afterwards.

Also, when it comes to Chinese restaurants, how come:

There are hundreds of dishes on the menu?

Horrible green peppers crop up everywhere?

You order a greater quantity of dishes than you would in any other sort of restaurant and then share them?

By the time any prawn dish gets round to you, there are no prawns left?

A complete meal can be prepared in five minutes?

There are never enough prawn toasts in the mixed hors d'oeuvres but no one wants to know the spring rolls?

Half a crispy duck is never as much food as two quarters of crispy duck – even though they cost the same?

They never serve enough cucumber or pancakes with the crispy duck?

You only stop eating when you're full to bursting?

You always feel hungry two hours later?

THE PERFECT RECIPE FOR THE CHRISTMAS FROM HELL

You turn on the TV to find a DJ going round the children's ward of a hospital.

The car packs up on the motorway.

Your in-laws decide that they can make it after all.

Someone insists on reading out every single Christmas cracker joke – and motto.

No one wants to eat the Brussels sprouts.

The children break all their presents before dinner.

Some people have spent too little on Christmas presents.

Some people have spent too much on Christmas presents.

The turkey's off.

Someone has used up all the tonic water as a soft drink.

There's a row over who gets to keep the Christmas cracker novelty.

The nutcrackers go AWOL.

Too many pairs of socks.

Too few volunteers for the washing-up.

You run out of Alka-Seltzer.

Two words: Christmas songs.

135

IRASCIBILITY

Tuition fees for students doing degrees in vocational subjects where there's a shortage of professional personnel.

Scots who support whoever's playing England at sport. It doesn't happen the other way round.

New medical cures always being at least ten years away.

Scantily clad women complaining that men are always staring at them.

Chain emails that threaten us with bad luck if we don't send them on.

People who don't bother to vote. If you can't vote for someone, make sure you vote against someone, but always always *always* vote. Otherwise you forfeit your right to complain until the next election.

People who bring up the past in arguments. Applies double to spouses.

Anyone who believes that crop circles are anything other than fakes. They are, you know. That's why they only appear in fields sited near large population areas (mostly in southern England) where a) the hoaxers obviously live and b) they'll be seen by the most people. Oh, and Father Christmas is your dad.

T-shirts that cost more than £20.

Not having a written Bill of Rights. Isn't it about time?

Sales that never have clothes in our size. All right: *my* size.

The 118 118 men – especially on satellite TV.

Has-been celebrities using charities to try to restart their careers.

Celebrities demanding our money for charity without putting their hands in their own pockets.

People who say 'I'm good' instead of 'I'm well' when asked how they are.

Lorry drivers who hog the fast lane of a dual carriageway all the way up a hill.

Gordon Brown's trust funds for kids. Why should we taxpayers hand over our hard-earned money for someone else's kids to blow it all in eighteen years' time?

Happy slappers. Wrong, wrong, wrong.

Unexplained – and, we suspect, unnecessary – train delays.

TV hypnotists. Wrong on so many levels.

Professional Scousers who don't live in Liverpool. Always going on about how great everyone is in Liverpool and how grounded they feel whenever they return. So why don't you live there all the year round? You never hear people who live in, say, Hampshire, going on about their county – even if they've never left there. (See also Professional Jocks and Professional Tykes.)

The government sanctioning house-building in the most built-up parts of the country.

Noisy neighbours in cities.

Being shouted at by double-glazing salesmen in TV commercials.

Parenting books – especially those written by celebrities. Haven't they heard of hubris?

Extracts from interviews on Sunday AM appearing on the news later on in the same programme.

Neighbours' cats fouling our gardens and killing birds in them. Why does society deem that acceptable?

Football managers with an overdeveloped sense of injustice but absolutely no sense of justice.

The people on *The Jeremy Kyle Show*. Especially Jeremy Kyle.

Former politicians turning to journalism. We've got enough unprincipled lying freeloaders, thank you very much.

People using phones while driving – even hands free. I want to know that the motorists who share *my* roads are paying full attention to their driving and not trying to close some deal or make detailed arrangements for the weekend. On the other hand, there's nothing wrong with someone who's (effectively) parked in a solid traffic jam picking up a phone to let the person who's expecting them know they're going to be late – and yet that's illegal.

Business gurus.

Grown men (and women) wearing replica football tops. Sad, so sad.

People who say 'sugar' or 'fudge' instead of swearing. Grow up, you country people.

Americans who pretend to be Irish – especially on St Patrick's Day.

Large companies – like supermarket chains – paying 17-year-olds less than 18-year-olds to do precisely the same jobs.

Selective quoting from reviews used in ads for films and plays. 'John Smith, who was so brilliant in his last play, gave an absolutely terrible performance in this one' becomes 'John Smith ... so brilliant'.

People who always trump your jokes. 'If you think *that's* funny...'

CAMRA. Campaign For Real Ale. Or should that be Can't Attract Miss Right Alas.

Fuel-station attendants who make us wait for ages before switching the pumps on.

Online poker players who call you a 'fish' just because you beat them with a hand that was initially weaker than theirs.

Actors who endlessly trade on a role in a TV soap or sitcom. That Tony Robinson out of *Blackadder* was down in Worthing earlier this year presenting his – wait for it – *Cunning Night Out*. And, no, I didn't go.

People who describe their tastes as 'eclectic' and their experiences as 'cathartic'.

Anyone who says that 'My Way' is 'their' song.

Tabloid newspapers that call Prince William 'Wills'. Stop being so damn familiar, you oiks.

REMEMBER WHEN...

People were actually arrested for being drunk and disorderly.

Women in their fifties became grandmothers – not mothers.

Women in their thirties became mothers – not grand-mothers.

Parking was free.

You could phone a business and speak to a person instead of a machine.

Olive oil was something you put in your ear – not on your salad.

Olive oil wasn't described as 'virgin' but girls were.

An AA Patrolman would salute you if your car had an AA badge.

Parents didn't swear at their children in public.

Dustmen would take your rubbish away – even if it wasn't in black plastic sacks.

You could call dustmen 'dustmen'.

All clergymen believed in God.

IRASCIBILITY

People with more than one mobile phone. 'Hang on, I'm just on the other phone.' Flash, self-important gits.

Sales assistants trying to sell us extended warranties. Especially annoying when the products in question cost less than fifty quid.

The expression 'letting go' as a euphemism for sacking someone.

Any poem by a Poet Laureate.

Government ministers who refuse to apologize.

People who keep big dogs in the inner cities.

Euro-fanatics. Wise up, guys. It's all been one massive costly mistake. Time to get out and cut our huge losses.

Ordinary footballers getting paid the equivalent of a year's salary every week. Am I the only person to notice the link between too much money and not enough morals? Time was when roasts were what footballers had on a Sunday for dinner – *with* their families.

Razorblade manufacturers always describing their latest product as 'the closest-ever shave'.

People who say 'no offence' just after they've been offensive.

People gobbing in the street. OK if it's absolutely essential but not when it's done gratuitously.

Firework fortnight. It's like the bloody Somme. Without the poets.

People who can eat whatever they like without getting fat.

Teenagers saying 'WHATEVER' to (almost) any question they're asked.

The idea that the Chancellor is giving his money to this or that. He's not: it's *our* money.

People who are so 'open-minded' about psychic phenomena that they always accept the daftest solution rather than the most obvious explanation.

Writers who use arcane language to show off.

People who dawdle across zebra crossings while talking on their mobile phones.

People who say 'Throwing it away now are we?' when you've dropped your change all over the floor.

Companies trademarking pathetic slogans – like 'Because we care'. NB I don't know if this actually is a trademarked slogan but you wouldn't want to bet against it.

Paying more duty on our fuel than Americans pay for the fuel itself.

Foreign oligarchs buying up our football clubs and transforming them into havens for mercenary footballers ('scuse the tautology).

Apple computer owners going on about how much they love their computers. Buying an Apple doesn't make you a good person any more than buying a Microsoft makes you a bad person. So stop being so annoyingly smug.

Meaningless awards ceremonies. Especially in the media. Best Use Of A Greek Olive In A Hairspray Advertisement? Well, you know what I mean.

Spam emails masquerading as personal ones: 'Hi Mitch, how are you?'

Ring-pulls on tins and cans that nearly sever your finger.

Cyclists who ride on the pavement and expect us to get out of their way.

The expression 'Been there, done that, got the T-shirt'. You haven't, you haven't, you haven't.

Lorries wrecking the kerbs of narrow streets.

Women who dye their hair blonde and then complain about 'blonde jokes'.

Warnings about 'strong language' before TV programmes starting after ten. Who the fuck's bothered?

Politicians making fools of themselves in their pathetic attempts to appeal to young people.

Huge lorries overtaking other huge lorries on two-lane motorways and dual carriageways.

'Sunday services' on public transport wherein the word 'services' is usually stretched beyond any possible definition of its meaning.

The silly prices charged for refreshments in multiplex cinemas.

TV interviewers interrupting politicians before they've had a chance to condemn themselves out of their own mouths.

Unfeasibly high postage charges on 'bargain' mail-order goods. Since when did £2.75 become the norm for paper-backs that cost half that to post?

The expression 'I hear what you're saying'. Almost always followed by the word 'but'.

People who park across two spaces in car parks.

Pricing policy in cinemas, which can lead to children paying more than (adult) students. Let's see. You're letting this hairy-arsed (I'm assuming) adult in for a reduced rate on the basis that he can prove – by dint of having an NUS card – that he's a full-time student. So why do you refuse to allow a 15-year-old boy who's obviously a full-time student – because, er, he's under 16 – to buy a cheaper ticket? Madness. And meanness.

More than one coffee shop in the high street. Each charging upwards of £3.00 for a coffee – and extra for a biscuit to go with it. Shouldn't the laws of the marketplace see prices lowered until one or more coffee shop goes under? Unless, of course (perish the thought), there's a cartel operating.

TV historians using the historical present ('so Sir Francis Drake carries on playing bowls before taking on the Spanish Armada').

Store cards with ludicrously high interest rates. 25 per cent over base is usury, nothing less.

Young men in slow cars driving too fast.

BBC TV sports presenters ignoring big matches to which they don't have the rights – or, worse, advising people to listen to them on Radio 5 – when they can be seen for free on ITV.

Companies that make you negotiate half a dozen telephone voice menus before you can speak to a human being.

Everything in life being seen or done through the prism of celebrities. There's nothing worse than dumb celebrities being asked for – and giving – their views on subjects about which they are pig ignorant.

Local councillors drawing wages as well as expenses. We really don't need yet another tier of paid politicians. Alas, it's all part of the aggrandizement of local government. The rot set in when the town clerk became the chief executive – on three times the salary.

Politicians talking about the NHS being 'free at the point of delivery'. And what does that mean?

'Baby On Board' – or, worse, 'Princess On Board' – car stickers. Oh, OK, I was going to drive into the back of your car but now I've seen that sign, I won't.

Traffic wardens who smile as they issue tickets.

Very senior police officers not getting banned for speeding offences.

Karaoke. Especially applies to anyone singing Sinatra songs.

THINGS THAT PARLIAMENT SHOULD BAN

MPs having paid outside interests (yes, Boris, even you).

Members of the prime minister's own party being allowed to ask (flattering) questions at Prime Minister's Questions.

MPs being self-employed when it comes to appointing wives and mistresses as secretaries and researchers but being treated as employees when it comes to pensions.

MPs are always banging on about how they're public servants – well, they should be treated like them, too. You don't get civil servants employing their wives and kids as secretaries and researchers – so why should politicians?

The ludicrously long breaks when Parliament is in recess (while the Executive is working, the Legislature should always be around to scrutinize it).

MPs talking about their 'consciences' (as if …).

MPs awarding themselves huge pay rises.

MPs justifying those pay rises on the grounds that they have to attract people to stand for Parliament – even though there's no shortage of candidates – while remaining curiously immune to extending the same principle to other professions like nursing or teaching.

Regional TV presenters milking their 'fame'.

Graffiti. Offenders should be forced to remove it. With their tongues.

So-called 'healthy' foods which replace fat with extra sugar and salt.

Groups of youths walking six abreast in high streets.

Disgraced politicians finding God. How quickly they absolve themselves.

English people always being embarrassed – even if they are in the right.

People who only ever complain, and never praise. For my own karma, I'd like to think that I praise staff, waiters, etc, twice as often as I criticize them.

Trying to get more than a couple of ice cubes in pubs. What's the matter? Is there a shortage of water or something?

Police officers driving at 28mph.

Car music systems with bass speakers that drown out every sound for miles around.

All nurses being described as 'angels'. Some and some.

Being told that 'shouting never solved anything' when we're, er, shouting.

Theatre actors milking applause after a particularly lousy play.

Noisy atonal music in clothes shops played by and for the staff.

Delivery men who don't turn up after we've taken the day off work to wait in for them.

Going down with a cold. The knowledge that the next seven days are going to pass miserably and slowly. Not ameliorated when we're told by our partners – with little feeling – that 'it's only a cold and not flu'.

Temporary speed reductions on motorways – even though the cause for them has long since vanished. Yet you can't drive at a sensible speed for fear that a police car will nick you for speeding.

Business class on European flights. Utterly pointless.

People who say they beat cancer because of some strange 'natural' product they bought off the internet when, in reality, it was the drugs and radiotherapy that did it. Ordinarily, such self-delusion wouldn't matter, but these people don't half proselytize and while there's any chance of cancer patients listening to them and discontinuing conventional treatment in favour of some quack remedy sold by a madwoman from South America, then we have a duty to shout them down.

Women who adopt African children as if they were pets.

Paparazzi stalking celebrities when they're not on offer – i.e. when they leave their homes, go on holiday, check into rehab, etc.

Celebrities complaining about the paparazzi hanging around outside places like the Ivy. Don't go there, dummy, if you don't want your picture taken.

Women who have their breasts enlarged and then still want to be treated as perfectly sensible human beings.

Actresses playing nurses earning more than real nurses. It's extraordinary when you stop to think about it.

Hotels with a bewildering array of rates, all expensive.

People who put pictures of their children on their Christmas cards and enclose a round-robin letter detailing their offspring's many achievements over the past twelve months.

TV newsreaders holding pens in a corny effort to persuade us that they write the news.

Best-before dates on bottles of natural spring water that has been gurgling underground for hundreds of years.

Local councils not sending Christmas cards for fear that it will offend people from ethnic minorities. It won't. Having said that, why would a local council want to waste ratepayers' money on sending Christmas cards anyway?

Foods that are obviously not high in fat – like Corn Flakes – being labelled as 'low fat'.

Drivers who don't indicate. Especially annoying at roundabouts.

Getting charged more than Americans for the same holiday. Even worse when the holiday is to be taken in Britain.

Litter on our streets.

Not daring to reproach people – especially yobs – for dropping litter.

People who refer to themselves as 'myself' instead of 'me'.

Cyclists ignoring the cycle paths that cost a fortune to install.

Pedants who insist on putting you right when you refer to our flag as the Union Jack.

TV programmes on ornithology and archaeology presented by actors and/or comedians.

Third World aid. In other words, poor people in rich countries giving money to rich people in poor countries. It's really not the answer.

Being told to call Third World countries 'developing countries'.

How To Speak 'Developing':

Developing. (Backward.)

Aid. (The president needs a new Gulfstream jet.)

Free election. (The results are freely available before the votes have been cast.)

Emergency relief. (Yup, it's another pop concert.)

Helping people to help themselves. (Selling beads to tourists.)

Indigenous culture. (*The Simpsons* dubbed in the local dialect.)

Western surpluses. (Dumping of high-tar cigarettes.)

Political amnesties. (Bodies released from jail for burial.)

Dartmoor ponies being exported for their meat.

Fire services have been instructed to take on more women. OK, nightmare scenario: you're woken in the night by thick smoke. You get out of bed and discover your home's on fire. Fortunately, you hear a fire engine. Now who do you want to see at your third-floor window? A big man or a petite woman? Precisely.

So what do women bring to the fire service? Feelings?
Political correctness is already stifling our lives: now it
threatens them, too. So can we just agree: some jobs
are too damn important to be subjected to petty –isms
like sexism. Save it for all the non-jobs advertised in
the *Guardian*.

Corporate automatons who are incapable of reasonable, independent thought, especially when faced with customer complaints.

Trinny and Tranny, the queens of Sneer TV.

Big Brother. It's not even bad TV, just CCTV.

Photographic studios that charge the thick end of a
grand to take some snapshots of the family – and then
won't even let their 'clients' keep them all.

Signs that say 'Please Drive Safely Through OUR Village' (it's
THE village if you don't want me putting my foot flat to the
floor as I drive through it). The community equivalent of
'baby on board' (qv).

People redeeming supermarket reward points at the
checkout – thereby holding up the queue.

European sports stars who speak English better than our
own sportsmen do. How shameful is that?

WHAT PR COMPANIES SAY TO PROSPECTIVE CLIENTS...

And What They Really Mean

'We can do a lot for your company's image.'
(You can do a lot for our company's bank account.)

'We have extensive experience in this field.'
(We've been fired by every one of your competitors.)

'You have to consider long-term strategy.'
(Please don't get rid of us after six months.)

'We often place our clients in *The Times*.'
(That's the *Brentford Times*.)

'We're a young firm and so we have to try that little bit harder.' (The girl who's looking after your account will also be making your tea today.)

'We will need to charge you for necessary expenses.'
(I've already reserved a regular table at the Ivy.)

'Remember, you have to get the right marketing mix.'
(Don't blame us – blame the advertising agency.)

'We don't have expensive offices.'
(Well, not until we receive your retainer.)

'I just know we're going to do some wonderful things together.' (Wimbledon, Lord's, Glyndebourne...I can't wait.)

People eating fast food in the street. We are meant to be superior to animals.

NIMBYs – especially when it comes to things that benefit society as a whole like bail hostels and units for the mentally ill.

High street shops that put placards out in the middle of the street for us to trip over.

Football chants at cricket games – especially 'Lancashire, la la la, Lancashire, la la la'.

'Infomercials' on the BBC telling us how reasonable the licence fee is.

Car-park attendants who pride themselves on not listening to excuses.

Being told to 'pull ourselves together' when we're off on one.

Women who wear 'funny' T-shirts and then complain that we chaps are staring at their breasts when we try to read them.

Built-in obsolescence. Goods built to last for precisely one day longer than the warranty.

The squitty boxy 'executive' rooms in the new wings of hotels. The rooms in the main part of the hotel are invariably bigger and have more character. They're also often cheaper – which is why the hotels sell you the 'executive' rooms.

Radio DJs who don't say what the record was that they were playing. Do you know what I mean? You switch on the radio in the middle of a song and you think: I like that, I wonder what it is so I can download it – legally, of course – off Napster. So you listen to the end of the song – just to hear the idiot DJ come up with some pathetic non-joke that he's only had three and a half minutes to think of.

Tom Baker's voiceovers. Past their use-by date.

CCTV cameras everywhere we go. Yes, I know, they come in useful when a child goes missing but there is something sinister about living in the most surveyed country in the world.

Advocates of alternative medicine who deny their children proper medical care.

Libraries spending their limited budgets on anything other than books (e.g. on DVDs and CDs).

Left-wing comics.

Right-wing comedians.

Men – it's always men – explaining films to their wives/girlfriends in cinemas.

Any woman buying a handbag that costs more than £200. Don't be silly, pet.

Having to do jury service. Why not have a panel of the unemployed/the retired/people who actually want to do it. I have no objection to doing *judge* service, however.

Train journeys that are more expensive than flights to the same destination. It's counter-intuitive.

Central reservations that are just too high to cross when you're in a traffic jam.

Restaurant waiters bringing expensive mineral water when we've asked for a jug of water.

AMERICAN TEENAGERS
– As Seen in Mainstream Hollywood Movies

They've all got cars.

They only see their parents at mealtimes.

They don't need sleep.

None of them smokes.

They're not obliged to wait at traffic lights.

Acne doesn't exist.

School attendance is optional past the age of twelve.

Even the poor ones are fabulously wealthy.

TV news reporters doing an item from a pub – e.g. on Budget Day – who hold up a glass and say 'cheers' at the end of their reports.

Market researchers. 'Can I just have a few minutes of your time?' Fuck off.

Baseball caps worn backwards.

Government ministers using the word stakeholder where taxpayer would be more accurate.

The Lotto TV studio audience cheering every number that's drawn. They can't ALL have won, surely?

Comic Relief. And all so that Lenny can get a gig.

TV ads louder than the programmes they punctuate.

TV companies denying that they're doing this.

The 'Intel inside' sting on every bloody TV ad for computers.

People – still – doing Vicky Pollard impersonations.

Supermarket checkout workers who put up the 'till closed' sign just when you reach the front of the queue.

Ex-public-schoolboy Phil Tufnell's Mockney accent. My mate Marcus went to Highgate School and he doesn't talk like a fucking costermonger.

People who wear football/rugby shirts they haven't played matches in.

Motorway lanes closed for 'roadworks' when there's no one actually doing any work.

Car parks which have a disproportionately high number of bays for disabled users – which doesn't mean that we shouldn't despise able-bodied people who park in disabled bays.

People who take too long at a cashpoint – i.e. doing anything other than drawing out cash – when there's a queue to use it.

Tattoos being called body art. Which makes you a canvas, you idiot.

Books about rotten Irish childhoods. Especially when exaggerated. That's to say, pretty well all of 'em.

The whooping of audiences on US TV sitcoms. *Nothing* is that funny.

People who are nice to you but are rude to waiters. Not a proper way to behave – although it is a remarkably useful 'tell'. The only two men I've known who were indeed rude to waiters also turned out to be the nastiest men I've ever known. If only I'd used the evidence that was available to me in those (respective) restaurants.

REALLY ANNOYING THINGS THAT MOTHERS SAY

'Would you *like* a smack?'

'I'll teach you to be disobedient.'

'You don't hear me talking to my parents like you talk to me.'

'And what time do you call this?'

'Stand still while I'm wiping your face!'

'We never had electronic toys.'

'Wait till your father gets home.'

Unapologetically communist 'comics' on Radio 4 panel shows. They wouldn't – quite rightly – have a BNP supporter on them so why have WRP members?

Misogynistic rappers.

Parents who dress their little daughters in 'sexy' T-shirts. Part of the wider problem of society's sexualization of children. Give 'em back their childhoods.

The words 'I told you so'. Never nice to hear.

Aggressive stupidity. Everyone is entitled to be stupid, but some people abuse the privilege.

The expression 'that's more than my job's worth' (even when used ironically).

Hot-air hand driers in public toilets. They might be more hygienic than a towel but the fact is they don't dry your hands. Which is, after all, the point.

'A **PERPETUAL** HOLIDAY
IS A GOOD WORKING DEFINITION
OF **HELL**.'

George Bernard Shaw

acked for easy assembly'. Why not t
e truth and say that they are in fa
at-packed for our own convenience a
e almost impossible to put togeth
nless you're a qualified carpenter
owever, if I'm honest, I've never actua
een to Ikea. I don't think it sounds li
y sort of place. Flagellating ourselv
r our supposed racism while we ta
ore asylum seeke any other
untry. Having when th
eather's g d. P say here
any worse you'
aving a surgeri
here you ... s b
ave to wa ould to se
ctor. who ha yo
ul ha giv the enti
te so e e The people
e sa -TV loan comp
ctur about ho
uch the £25,000? Ye
at fine. morons wou
ak up t ow much th
an d th hile they we
tual e pho and those a
idently th sort of c tomers Pictu
ants. There's a further reason to ha
cture: they use the music from the o
show Vision On – thereby spoiling
r ever. Come to think of it though,
as a bit strange having such brillia
eme music for a show that was aime
, er, deaf children. Was the idea th
eir hearing siblings would sign to the
ou're missing such a great tune, y

OUTRAGE

Having to wait longer each year for Tax Freedom Day – the notional day when we start working for ourselves and not for the government.

Estate agents treating buyers – rather than sellers – as their clients.

Politicians assuming that we are all stupid. They do, you know.

Neighbours' visitors who sound their car horns when leaving. Makes me wish I hadn't surrendered that AK47 in the last amnesty.

Drivers driving slowly in the middle lane on motorways when the inside lane is empty.

People who pronounce the letter 'h' as 'haitch'.

Paying more (per litre) in pubs for soft drinks than alcohol.

Comics getting easy laughs with anti-Bush jokes. The easier the target, the harder you've got to work.

Spice Girls reunion. Just the thought of it makes me feel depressed. I hate them all – except Emma Bunton.

New Year's Eve. It's a loathsome occasion that brings out all the amateur revellers who are miserable sods for the rest of the year. For ugly blokes, it's an even better opportunity than the company Christmas party to inflict their beery bad breath on any unfortunate women who happen to get in their way as Big Ben chimes twelve. And I'd rather listen to a hundred karaoke singers murdering 'My Way' than a single drunken rendition of the maudlin' 'Auld Lang Syne'. The only New Year's resolution I ever make is to ignore New Year's Eve. And I always keep my resolution.

Hotel receptionists working in Britain for whom English isn't even a second language. We're not racist for saying it: just desperate.

People who call university 'uni'. This applies especially to people who didn't go to university themselves but whose offspring have applied to some former poly posing as a university.

Yobs who know their rights but not their responsibilities.

English football supporters who pronounce their country's name with three syllables – Eng-er-land. Interesting crossover with men whose knuckles scrape the pavement when they walk.

People in car parks who walk behind our cars when we're reversing. What are you? 1/64th hedgehog?

Visible thongs. Especially on fat birds.

Deliberately unsilenced car and motorbike exhausts.

Paying over the odds for CDs and DVDs. And don't tell us how expensive they are to produce because they fall out of our newspapers every weekend.

Sitting in a traffic jam while police outriders escort minor royals to the airport so that they can go swanning off on yet another free jaunt.

Ikea or any store that sells goods 'flat-packed for easy assembly'. Why not tell the truth and say that they are in fact 'flat-packed for our own convenience and are almost impossible to put together unless you're a qualified carpenter'? However, if I'm honest, I've never actually been to Ikea. I don't think it sounds like my sort of place.

Flagellating ourselves for our supposed racism while we take more asylum seekers than any other EU country.

Having to work when the weather's good.

People who say 'there's many worse off than you' when you're having a whinge.

Doctors' surgeries where you can't book appointments but have to wait for up to an hour to see a doctor.

Shop assistants who hand you your change while giving their entire attention to someone else.

The people in the satellite-TV ad for the loan company Picture who are so cavalier about how much they're borrowing. '£25,000? Yes, that's fine.' Only complete morons would make up their minds how much they wanted to borrow while they were actually on the phone and those are evidently the sort of customers Picture wants. There's a further reason to hate Picture: they use the music from the old TV show *Vision On* – thereby spoiling it for ever. Come to think of it though, it was a bit strange having such brilliant theme music for a show that was aimed at, er, deaf children. Was the idea that their hearing siblings would sign to them, 'You're missing such a great tune, you lugless wretch'?

Government thinking of ever more unbelievable ways to tax motorists...

...and using the environment as its justification.

The advertising slogan 'Because I'm worth it'. Grrr...

The word 'community' used to describe groups of people who are not especially communal – e.g. the shoplifting community, the speeding community, the dogging community (actually, they probably *could* be described as a community).

Teenage girls who, without any means of support, exercise their right to have a 'baybee'. The difference between a baby and a 'baybee' is that whereas a baby is for life, a 'baybee' is basically a glorified pet to be discarded (or left to run wild) as soon as the mother is bored or is distracted by more 'baybees'. Most girls who get pregnant aged sixteen or under end up being cared for by us. We pay for it now and we pay for it again in sixteen years' time when the 'baybee' girls become pregnant themselves and the 'baybee' boys, brought up without proper parental discipline, turn to crime.

The default option for pregnant minors should be abortion or, if their religion precludes that, adoption. No single teenage mother should be given housing accommodation. If they choose to keep their child, all they should be able to expect is a place in a mother-and-baby hostel – no matter how many babies they subsequently have. Parents, teachers and other authority figures should stop biting their lips and start talking tough love. A friend of mine was, until recently, a school nurse. She was appalled by the number of teenage mothers, but worse was the teachers' attitude to them. Instead of chiding them, they made a big fuss of them and their 'baybees'. What message does this approval send to the other pupils? Illegitimate children used to be known as bastards. That was wrong but the pendulum has swung too far in the opposite direction. 'Bastard' is a much harsher word than 'baybee' but it does at least carry some much-needed stigma, which is something that silly girls desperately need if they are to be deterred from ruining their silly lives.

Being asked to rate *every* transaction we do on the internet. 'Mitchell Symons, will you share your experience? Help the Amazon Marketplace community by rating your recent transaction.' It was only a bleeding book purchase, not a fortnight's holiday.

Restaurants that don't pass on all the tips to the waiters and waitresses. You should always check before putting it on the credit card. If they don't, then make sure you give them their tip in cash.

Added salt in sweet foods.

Added sugar in savoury foods.

Faith schools – especially state faith schools. I'd ban the lot.

People asking us to sponsor them to do things they'd happily do even if they weren't raising money for charity.

Noisy, drunken people overspilling from pubs on to the pavement. Especially in summer.

BBC bias. Don't get me started. All right do. So long as you're on the right side, which at the BBC means anti-America, anti-Israel, pro-abortion, anti-religion (unless it's a foreign one in which case you have to 'respect their culture'), anti-capital punishment, pro-immigration, you're guaranteed to be safely cosseted in Auntie's capacious bosom. I suppose it's understandable that people who got their jobs through the *Guardian*'s

media ads should be *Guardian* readers and have *Guardian* views. Maybe the answer is to advertise BBC jobs throughout the media. Same goes for jobs in the social services.

Celebrity chefs. Get back in your kitchens, you fame junkies.

All of this government's stealth taxes.

British internet sites selling British products or services that ask us for our zip codes and then make us scroll down a long list of countries till we find the United Kingdom.

Beggars sitting next to cash machines. Why do you never have an electric cattle prod when you need one?

Inflation-busting rises in things we're obliged to pay for – like council tax, utility bills and train fares.

Rock stars' ludicrous concert demands. Why would anyone need their M&Ms separated by colour? Unless it's for the same reason that dogs lick their balls – because they can.

Mobile phone conversations held at full volume on public transport. We know you're on the train because we too are on the train. As for the person you're talking to, do they really *need* to know? I mean, you haven't just tunnelled out of Stalag Luft III in *The Great Escape*, have you?

Russian gangsters abroad. Loud, flash, aggressive and boorish. But who's going to tell them?

OUTRAGE

HOLIDAY BROCHURES:
What They Say… And What They Really Mean

'This resort is popular with all nationalities.'
(Don't even *think* of getting a seat by the pool.)

'Enjoy the local culture.' (British pubs with satellite TVs.)

'Only fifteen minutes from the beach.'
(Fifteen minutes by motorway.)

'The hotel is brand new.'
(And the swimming pool will be ready any day now.)

'This bustling town…'
(Make sure your valuables are well insured.)

'…with its exciting nightlife.'
(British teenagers vomiting in the streets at midnight.)

'For your peace of mind we have a representative who is always available.' (Particularly if you're young and fit.)

'The hotel is well established.'
(The local health inspectors know the manager by name.)

'The island is totally unspoilt.'
(No point in asking for a doctor when you get
food poisoning.)

TV programmes that constantly trail what's coming up later in the programme so that by the time the constantly trailed item does indeed 'come up', you feel like you've already seen it. Even more annoying when they regularly repeat what you've already seen.

'Recovering alcoholics' who can't shut up about their alcoholism. Attending six AA meetings a week isn't necessarily better than drinking a bottle of vodka a day.

Astrology. It's not a science. Indeed, the only scientific fact that can be learnt from the whole parcel of bollocks is that at any gathering of people, it'll be the dopiest bird present who asks you what your star sign is. Since the dopiest bird isn't necessarily the ugliest, it might be worthwhile to let her down gently. However, give ugly women and – especially – blokes who attempt to engage you on the subject both barrels…

…which leads me neatly on to newspaper astrologers. Far be it from me to cry foul over these scamsters as I have been known to sail pretty close to the wind myself. (Least said, soonest mended.) So good luck to them as they rack up zillions on their premium phone lines from daft women. But they must *know* that it's total crap. What gets me is that these people – the astrologers, not the d.w. – are so difficult to pin down: it's like trying to juggle gravy. How, you say, can the entire world be divided up into twelve groups? Well, they reply, they don't: it's all about rising signs and

specific times and the conjunction of planets and so on – till your eyes glaze over and you're about to give up when you suddenly say, oi, wait a minute: if that's the case, then how do you still manage to publish a daily horoscope that's supposedly applicable to a twelfth of the population? At which point they go all smug and start talking about general characteristics etc etc. That's when you realize that they really are shameless scamsters who deserve to have their skulls battered like Canadian harp seals and that, yes, gravy-juggling is indeed preferable to debating with them.

TV news double acts in which each presenter can only manage very short sentences and the other presenter has to pick up from the last sentence by saying 'yes' or 'yes indeed'.

Anti-Americans. In the history of the world – from Ancient Rome to the British Empire – there has never been such a benign superpower. It can't be said too often – or too loudly – that America is not what's wrong with the world.

People who want to share their religious or political views with you but who don't want you to share yours with them. Just try explaining your belief in Satanism to the Jehovah's Witness couple on your doorstop. You won't convince them.

Car boot sales as havens for people fencing stolen goods. Anyone selling more than one ripped-out car radio at a car boot sale is almost certainly selling stolen goods. Same goes with razorblades which are, apparently, the most stolen items from high street

shops. Where else would thieves get rid of them if not at car boot sales? I also have an anecdotal experience to add. When our garden shed was broken into and a few things were nicked, the policeman we reported it to told us that if we wanted to see our property again, we should go to the local car boot sale. He meant it ruefully but it does raise the question: why don't the police themselves go to car boot sales? They could take along details of what's been stolen in the past few months. At the very least, they could ask traders just how they happen to have more than one ripped-out car stereo for sale. Their presence alone would deter the criminals. As for the cost of police presence, let the landowner pay. Down here in Sussex, farmers rake in up to £4,000 a week for fields that are already bringing them in thousands in EU set-aside. Time was when car boot sales gave people the opportunity to get rid of unwanted clutter and to make a few bob to buy some more. There are still people like that at car boot sales and, if you're one of them, good luck to you, but take a careful look at the bloke who's got the pitch next to you. He might be flogging your neighbour's most cherished possessions. Next week, he could be selling yours.

The Human Rights Act. Always seems to work at the expense of *our* human rights.

Thin people complaining how fat they are.

20mph speed limits outside schools still applying at midnight.

Junk mail offering us loans. Just in the past week, I've been invited to 'remortgage and unlock the extra cash tied up in your home'. Worried that I was paying 'too much' for my 'personal loan', another company offered me an 'Express Loan' – advertised as 'The solution that could save you money'. Yet another bank wrote to me declaring, 'No credit? No problem! A chance to build your credit history' – and, at a minimum 15.7 per cent APR, I could indeed be sure of a long credit history – while there were other offers of credit cards from, among others, the company that supplies my stationery (or at least did until they decided to try to flog me financial products too). Not one of these communications was solicited by me and just the credit card limits alone would allow me to rack up hundreds of thousands of pounds' worth of debt. And that's when it starts to hurt. Oh, sure, there's no interest for a short honeymoon period but, after that – assuming I couldn't be bothered to transfer my balance – they'd fix me up with a double-figure APR. Time was when 'debt' was a dirty word: now it's a lifestyle choice. Pop into your nearest department store and you'll see the staff tripping over themselves to offer charge cards – at 20 or 30 points above base rate – to people whose propensity to gorge themselves on debt is matched only by their inability to manage their finances. Alternatively, turn on the telly – even during children's programmes – just so that they too can be 'educated' in the ways of live now, pay for ever after – and you too will be asked: Need a low-cost loan at YOUR convenience? Want to clear your debts and reduce your monthly outgoings? Why not consolidate all your

outstanding loans into one easy monthly payment? You might even have enough left over to treat yourself to that holiday you deserve! You and I might believe that no one 'deserves' a holiday for which they haven't saved but then we're not part of the 'me' generation who sneer at thrift, baulk at abstinence and are mystified by any notion of deferred gratification. They want what they want and they want it NOW. And then they want more. They'll only start to worry when their credit cards are taken away and they find themselves in the county court. But even then, there's a solution. 'CCJs? No worries! We can still give you that loan you need.' And indeed there are no worries – until the dizzyingly high interest rates offered to these wretches start to bite. For it's a sad fact of life that the people who can least afford high rates of interest are the ones who are doomed to pay them. Those of us lucky enough not to inhabit this twilight world of CCJs and unmanageable debt shouldn't be feeling too smug because when the crash happens, it will precipitate a recession that will affect us all. Expecting voracious lenders to show voluntary restraint is pointless. They must be regulated so that they're stopped from sucking vulnerable people into a vortex of debt. Young consumers should be encouraged to save before they spend and they should be educated in the joys of negotiating cash discounts. And the rest of us should chuck junk mail in the bin where it belongs.

Lawyers who get their rich clients off speeding or drink/drive charges on technicalities.

Men on stag nights.

Very ordinary plays that receive rave reviews. I know that one of the qualifications for being a theatre reviewer is a love of theatre but they should remember that they're meant to be on *our* side.

Traffic calming measures. I never find them particularly calming.

Anyone who doubts the decision to drop atomic bombs on Japan in World War 2. Don't take my word for it – just ask any POW. Any POW, that is, who managed to survive the Japs.

Anyone who doubts the decision to bomb Dresden in World War 2. We didn't start the fire.

Jobsworths with absolutely zero common sense.

Probation officers referring to ex-prisoners as 'clients'.

Apologists for spies like Burgess, Maclean, Philby and Blunt who betrayed us to the communists.

Loan sharks. A manifestation of our spiv economy.

Cashback on loans and mortgages. Another manifestation of our spiv economy.

Wim Wenders' films. Especially *Lightning Over Water*, which made me want to kick Wenders in the throat.

People shooting wildlife in the name of 'sport'. It's only sport if the wildlife have guns, too.

Having to hold in farts in public. We know – from *Why Girls Can't Throw* (available in etc. etc.) that it's not dangerous but that doesn't make it any easier.

Our favourite bands letting us down.

Companies which employ people for whom English is not their first language as telephone operators.

Otherwise good internet sites – like Lastminute.com – that don't list their phone number so you can't query or change anything.

Otherwise good internet sites – like Lastminute.com – that don't list their phone number so you can't query or change anything but which have a list of FAQs. And guess what? Those too don't feature the phone numbers…

Micro-celebrities who do anything to get themselves noticed – then complain about the invasion of their privacy.

70mph motorway speed limits for cars that can cruise comfortably at 100mph.

Public toilets that don't have toilet paper.

Secretaries and PAs who protect their bosses from people they really should be speaking to. People like you and me … So don't tell me he's in a meeting, pet, when you and I both know that the creep is sitting in the same office as you.

Airport taxes (and airport taxis while we're at it: outrageously expensive). How dare they charge us to leave the country? Same goes for the price of passports going up by much more than the rate of inflation. Even the cost of escaping the nightmare that is modern Britain is increasing.

Clothes shops boasting 'up to 70 per cent off' when 99 per cent of the goods are just 10 per cent off.

Fifty-something female politicians being described in the press as 'babes'. Yeah, I know it's relative but even so…

Rizla manufacturing giant cigarette papers for the use of cannabis smokers.

People who support football teams because it's fashionable or, in the case of politicians or businessmen, expedient to do so.

BONFIRE NIGHT:
Annoying Things That Happen Every Year

The taper that comes with the box of fireworks doesn't light.

There isn't a bottle for the rockets.

The person who goes on most about the Firework Code is the first to relight the firework that didn't go off.

The firework you keep till the end for the grand finale turns out to be useless.

The tomato soup boils over.

The sausages you cook on the bonfire get burned on the outside while remaining raw on the inside.

The Catherine Wheel flies off the tree as soon as it starts spinning.

The guy falls apart at the precise moment when he's too hot to be remade.

Next door's display is always better than yours.

Everyone agrees that it was a complete waste of money.

People taking offence on behalf of other people. No one – not Jews, nor Muslims, nor Sikhs – objects to hot cross buns at Easter so there's really no need to be so concerned. Or is it that you're actually getting off on it, you nasty interfering pieces of work?

The M4 bus lane.

High street banks pretending to be different from each other.

Able-bodied men – and women – who don't stand up for pregnant women on public transport.

Government aides and advisors making a fortune out of their diaries/memoirs/autobiographies. Just because it's in a book and not in a red-top tabloid doesn't make it any less of a betrayal of former colleagues.

People acting boorishly in public swimming pools. That's always the justification for the people who run the pools to have 'women only' sessions. That's unnecessary: they should hold 'properly behaved people only' sessions – all the time.

Sending financial aid to countries that squander their own money on nuclear missile programmes. Someone should tell these countries to get their priorities right. And someone should tell our government the same.

Teenage yobs demanding money with menaces on Halloween.

The periodic message – spoken by a posh actress who sounds nothing like any of the operators – telling us how much the big company that's keeping us hanging on the phone values our custom.

Giving money to a charity and then receiving letters from them asking for more money.

Prince Andrew using the royal jet to fly to Scotland for the golf. Still, so long as he enjoys himself, eh?

Art critics giving intellectual succour to pretentious and meaningless works of modern art.

Proposals to cancel Third World debt. It only punishes the prudent.

People who shout at night when passing our front doors.

Dog owners who watch their dogs pooing in parks and then don't clear it up.

Telephone canvassers. 'We're not trying to sell you anything…' Yes you are. 'We're not…' Yes you ARE. 'We're installing kitchens in your area and we wanted to know…' If I wanted to buy a kitchen. 'Well, yes.' So why did you say you weren't trying to sell me anything? 'Because you would have put the phone down.' Which is what I'm going to do now. Click.

MURPHY'S LAW

Anything that can go wrong will go wrong.

When someone says, 'It's not the money, it's the principle', nine times out of ten it's the money.

As soon as you mention something: a) if it's good, it goes away; b) if it's bad, it happens.

When the train you are on is late, the bus to take you home from the station will be on time.

The odds of the bread falling butter-side down are directly proportional to the value of the carpet.

If during a month only three enjoyable social activities take place, they will all happen on the same evening.

The first place to look for something is the last place you would expect to find it.

Whenever you make a journey by bicycle, it's always more uphill than downhill.

You never find something until you replace it.

If an experiment works, something has gone wrong.

When you dial a wrong number, it is never engaged.

In a supermarket, the other queues always move faster than yours.

Friends come and go but enemies accumulate.

The severity of an itch is inversely proportional to how easy it is to scratch it.

Motorists who throw lit cigarette ends out of moving cars or – just as bad – empty their ashtrays in car parks.

Products made and sold in Britain with information printed in eight languages.

Homoeopathy. It doesn't work. IT DOESN'T WORK. IT DOESN'T WORK.

Hotels that offer you a higher rate than you can get on the internet – while swearing blind that this really is their cheapest rate.

Supposedly witty car stickers that obscure drivers' views.

Antisocial teenage offenders who can't be named 'for legal reasons', which are, of course, precisely the reasons why they *should* be named.

Golf clubs banning women from playing at certain times.

Professional beggars who abuse you when you refuse to hand over your hard-earned money.

Touts who buy up all the tickets to see our favourite stars and then flog them to us for ridiculous sums – thereby creating the demand as well as satisfying it.

Supporters who make a fetish of their football teams. There is nothing more disturbing than the sight of a grown man weeping because 'his' club has lost a football game. The clue's in the word 'game', saddo.

OUTRAGE

The veneration of crusty old politicians like Tony Benn. Just because they're coffin dodgers doesn't automatically make them great blokes.

The abolition of regiments and infantry battalions. These units are formidable fighting families which we lose at our peril. It's strange that a government that sees everyone in terms of 'communities' – no matter how spurious – seems uncommonly keen to scrap genuine communities that serve the widest community of all – the British public.

Legal aid for wealthy people in civil actions.

Organizations like schools' Parents' Associations having to go to the magistrates' court and apply for a licence before they can sell wine or beer at fund-raising events attended only by adults. Contrast that with teenagers in city centres openly smoking dope and almost as openly dealing drugs.

Public footpaths that are closed to the public.

People who allow their cats to roam the streets at night. And then complain when they're run over.

People opening car doors into oncoming traffic.

'Courtesy calls' which are anything but courteous.

186

People who drive at precisely 70mph in the fast lane of the motorway.

MPs having more than one job. Simply shouldn't be allowed. Made even worse by MPs claiming that it gives them 'important experience of the real world'. Greedy scrotes.

The EU. All you need to know about it is that it's a trade-off between France and Germany to ensure French security and German power. It's a private arrangement and we shouldn't be having anything to do with it. The fact is, if there's any point in being part of a single Europe, it's that we should get the benefits as well as the burdens. It never seems to work that way. We get the Brussels directives and the VAT increases 'to bring us into line with Europe' but it is still cheaper to buy a bottle of Scotch in Spain than it is in Scotland. And if our government is so keen for us to move at the same pace as the rest of Europe, how about increasing the speed limit on our motorways?

The wasting of vast sums of our money on logos and slogans for public bodies that simply state the bleeding obvious (e.g. 'Metropolitan Police. Working for a safer London').

Static electricity shocks. Especially in hotel corridors.

People who call drugs by their nicknames (e.g. junk, toot, Mary Jane).

Cults that masquerade as legitimate religions.

People who say 'could of' and 'would of' instead of 'could have' and 'would have'.

Utilities increasing their prices above the rate of inflation. There was never any point in privatization if the utilities were going to remain monopolies.

Any woman who refers to her shoes by brand – 'I can't live without my Jimmy Choos/Manolo Blahniks'. Invariably the sort of woman who used to say 'I can't live without my Prada (handbag)'. Worth having a communist revolution just for them.

Visible vomit in films and TV dramas.

Health 'n' Safety officials with absolutely *no* sense of proportion. It probably isn't possible to remove *all* risk and even if it were, what kind of world would it be?

People boasting to us about how often they go to the gym. So you're going to live forever and we're going to die tomorrow? Happy now?

People going on about their – or, more likely, *our* – 'Carbon footprints'.

Cyclists with no lights dressed in dark clothing cycling at night. How come the law doesn't protect them from their own stupidity like it does with car drivers and passengers who, quite rightly, are obliged to wear safety belts? Couldn't have anything to do with the fact that drivers are easy to trace, could it? Thought so.

THE LAWS OF COMMITTEES

'Any other business' takes longer than all the other items on the agenda put together.

The dullest member of the committee will always do the most speaking.

Any committee which cannot agree on the minutes of the last meeting is doomed to break up – in tears – within three months.

The amount of time spent debating subjects is in inverse proportion to their importance.

The secretary is always the hardest-working person on any committee.

The vice-chairman is always the laziest person on any committee.

Whatever the purpose of a committee, if it has more than one meeting a month, the meetings become more important than its purpose.

If you're friends with someone before you both serve on the same committee, you won't be afterwards.

It needs all the committee members to make committee meetings enjoyable; it only needs one committee member to make committee meetings hellish.

Overbearing officiousness in the name of security.

Women wearing fur because they think it's fashionable.

Chewing-gum on the pavement.

Squatters and their 'rights'. What about the rights of homeowners?

Booze companies and supermarkets that sell booze claiming to support 'responsible drinking' when it's clear that they make their (huge) profits from *irresponsible* drinking.

Ambitious, pushy, middle-class parents who have to find a condition or a syndrome to mitigate their thick children's lack of academic ability.

Filthy London Underground train carriages.

Shop assistants carrying on a conversation with their mate(s) while ostensibly serving us.

Rock stars' kids latching on to their fathers' names to become famous.

Ridiculously predatory elderly repulsive homosexuals. I'm thinking of the late Frankie Howerd who once told me that he could – and I quote – 'stick my cock up your arse any time'. I told him that the BBC didn't pay me enough.

The high jump – and vaulting horses. The bane of any fat lad's childhood.

The French. When God created France, He realized that He had gone overboard in creating the most perfect place on Earth. So to balance it out, he created the French people.

Facial hair on women.

Curries of dodgy provenance. Why don't we – damn it *I* – learn our lesson.

US immigration officials treating British tourists as suspicious aliens rather than as welcome guests. What about the Special Relationship?

People who don't own a TV 'on principle'. I always ignore them 'on principle'.

Lobby journalists. Oh how they love living in the Westminster Village in a world of non-attributable briefings. Doesn't take long for them to go native so they should be replaced every year before they forget who pays their wages.

'MAYBE THIS WORLD IS ANOTHER PLANET'S HELL.'

Aldous Huxley

ere with 'the environment'. I am so s
f being hectored and berated by ec
scists who accuse me and people li
e of being responsible for an area
mazonian jungle the size of Wales – w
it always the size of Wales? – getti
hopped down every year, even thou
e truth is that emissions from all t
orld's cars are meaningless compared
e damage done by forest fires and
ws parping. The night, the metha
roduced from a far worse th
ny cataly and CO2 emitt
om my Saab that
isn't so qui
nyway, global
rming? the ice-cap melt an
e get to the M summer
builds a fa me. Vendi
achines that ense wh
ou've just paid for. infu
ing by the peopl
orking on-site to bili
he machine, noth B
's on your prem but i
wned by a s company.' So wh
m I supposed to do? 'You have to wri
the company.' Yeah, right TV a
viting people to claim for 'com-pen-sa
un'. 'Where there's blame, there's
aim' – yeah and where there's a po
cker, there's a greedy fucker... Jan
reet-Porter. Should have her vocal cor
rcibly removed. Being woken up by
rong number at four in the mornin
hen we have to be up at six. Micha

FURY

The Princess of Wales's former staff still cashing in on her memory. Yes, Burrell, I'm talking about you. The cad Hewitt might have slept with her but you're the creep who's screwing her – or, at least, her memory.

The State interfering in our lives whenever it can. It should only do so when absolutely necessary. Alas, nothing is going to change until a politician has the bravery to tackle the special-interest groups that have infiltrated our country to such an extent that they've become the new Establishment. Political correctness is their watchword and the *Guardian* is their bible. They define themselves not by what they love but by what they hate, and it's a long list headed by their own country, McDonald's, individuality, multinationals, cars and, above all, America. Mock them as we do, they have nevertheless shifted the paradigm. It's thanks to these people that we can't deport illegal immigrants posing as 'asylum seekers' without fear of being labelled racists; it's thanks to these people that traditional British customs are being eroded in the name of

'multiculturalism'; it's thanks to these people that the police, courts and probation service treat motorists as criminals and criminals as clients. The world we used to know has gone and it's never coming back.

NHS hospital car-parking charges – ruthlessly enforced by private contractors. There was a story in the papers about a bloke whose wife had just died in A&E and his car was clamped in the car park. And, no, the clampers didn't think that was an acceptable excuse.

Being welcomed to places one has no wish to be in and thanked for doing things one has no wish to do. For example: 'Welcome to the car pound'; 'Thank you for paying the Congestion Charge'.

Soviet-style communists in the countries that made up the USSR. Do these people never learn?

Government ministers who apologize but refuse to resign.

The end of British Summer Time: let's have it all year round and sod the Scottish farmers.

The environment. I have had it right up to here with 'the environment'. I am so sick of being hectored and berated by eco-fascists who accuse me and people like me of being responsible for an area of Amazonian

jungle the size of Wales – why is it always the size of Wales? – getting chopped down every year, even though the truth is that emissions from all the world's cars are meaningless compared to the damage done by forest fires and by cows parping. That's right, the methane produced from a cow is far worse than any catalytically converted CO_2 emitted from my Saab 95 but try telling that to Daisy because she doesn't do guilt. Anyway, what's the deal with global warming? So the polar ice-caps melt and we get to have Mediterranean summers? Sounds a fair trade to me.

Vending machines that don't dispense what you've just paid for. Made more infuriating by the refusal of the person/people working on-site to take responsibility. 'The machine's nothing to do with us.' But it's on your premises. 'Yeah, but it's owned by a separate company.' So what am I supposed to do? 'You have to write to the company.' Yeah, right.

TV ads inviting people to claim for 'com-pen-say-shun'. 'Where there's blame, there's a claim' – yeah and where there's a poor sucker, there's a greedy fucker…

Janet Street-Porter. Should have her vocal cords forcibly removed.

Being woken up by a wrong number at four in the morning when we have to be up at six.

 FURY

Restaurants putting a 300 per cent mark-up on wine. Totally unjustified given that they don't actually have to *do* anything to the wine. Even worse is when they have the nerve to charge service on top of their ludicrous mark-up.

People who don't flush public toilets.

Giant sheets at roundabouts to 'celebrate' people's birthdays. There are poster sites, you know, where you can PAY to mark a loved one's landmark birthday. I find that my anger increases in line with the age of the person being celebrated. If they're eighteen or twenty-one then it's merely annoying, but if they're fifty or sixty, then they should know how totally tragic their lives are – how little they've amounted to – that that's how their birthday is being marked.

Tobacco-company executives still claiming that smoking doesn't cause lung cancer. Just adds insult to injury.

Al Gore. The opportunist's opportunist. *An Inconvenient Truth* might very well be an extremely convenient platform for him to launch a presidential bid. I'm writing this in the summer of 2007 when he's not even a candidate. If you happen to be reading this after November 2008, you'll know how prescient I was. Or not.

Politicians resigning as ministers or front-bench spokesmen but *not* as MPs after finding themselves exposed as liars/cheats/slags in the red-tops.

Victoria Beckham's pout. I'm against violence to women on principle but never have I seen a face more in need of a slap.

Congestion charging. Why should I have to pay to drive my car (bought out of taxed income with VAT charged on the purchase) which runs on fuel carrying 80 per cent tax into the capital of the country which I just happen support through my taxes?

Door-to-door salesmen flogging dusters at three quid a go. 'I'm unemployed and trying to do my best to earn a little money...' No you're not. You're a skanky little chancer who's earning a fortune for a drug-dealing, whore-pimping scumbag in the Midlands who busses down hundreds of toerags just like you to rip off middle-class suburban householders too guilty/scared to say no. Now fuck off and get yourself a proper job, you piece of shit.

Employers who take advantage of interns by making them work all hours for no pay – even when there's no prospect of a job for them at the end of it.

Politicians who refuse to give direct answers to questions put to them by interviewers. The ONLY way to interview politicians is with electrodes applied to their genitals.

Having to pay for directory enquiries. The fact is that ever since British Telecom – in a disgraceful disavowal of its public service remit – started charging for its 'service',

we've learned to do without directory enquiries unless there really is no alternative. We've got their number. And, no, we're not going to phone it.

Intimidating animal-rights activists who use violence to achieve their often ill-judged ends.

People who don't tax, insure or have MOTs for their cars. And then crash. Into those of us who *do* tax, insure and have MOTs for our cars.

MPs fiddling their expenses and not getting punished for it.

Train passengers being forced to take buses for part of their journeys. When we buy train tickets, we expect to be taken all the way – by *train*. In the unlikely event that we want to get off halfway and get on a bus, we're perfectly capable of arranging it ourselves.

Having to speak to call centres in India when we're trying to sort out an insurance claim for something that happened in Britain.

Ex-pats who criticize Britain without paying their taxes here. They have less right to do that than the skankiest illegal immigrant working cash-in-hand who is at least paying *some* tax through the things he can't avoid buying.

Public drunkenness – especially teenage public drunkenness. Why have the police sold the pass on this?

Satellite TV adverts for injury claim lawyers. 'And will I get to keep *all* the money?' Oh *yes*. 'Does that mean you'll be working *pro bono*?' Er, not exactly.

Overcrowding in prisons. Prisons are there to punish criminals, deter other criminals and protect the public. I don't think it's inconsistent to believe that they should also adhere to minimum sanitary standards. Basic humanity demands nothing less. Tough on crime: tough on the causes of grime. If one of the objectives of prison is to rehabilitate and cut reoffending, then it's clearly not working. Could overcrowding be part of the problem? Even if it isn't – and it is – it's still shameful in a supposedly civilized country to be banging up prisoners three to a cell designed by illiberal Victorians for single occupancy. The bottom line is that we need to have enough prisons to house all the people who need to be imprisoned – in single cells. We also need to have enough prison warders to look after them and enough teachers/lecturers/instructors to rehabilitate them. If that means more expenditure then so be it. The alternatives are simply unacceptable.

People who encourage younger people to use cannabis – despite all the medical evidence of the mental problems it can lead to. And is there anything worse than hearing a man over the age of forty talking about 'the munchies'?

Politicians. As e.e. cummings said, 'A politician is an arse upon which everyone has sat except a man.' They believe in nothing except themselves and their careers.

Ten Commandments for Politicians:

1. Thou shalt have no other Gods before Power, Greed and Naked Ambition.

2. Thou shalt make unto thee any graven image-maker if thou intends to appear on TV.

3. Thou shalt not take the name of thy party leader in vain.

4. Remember the Sabbath day and use it to meet thy constituents lest thou be de-selected.

5. Honour thy Chief Whip that thy days in Parliament may be long and free from nagging.

6. Thou shalt not kill bills which thy front bench has put before the house.

7. Thou shalt not commit adultery with anyone who knows the telephone number of the *News of the World*.

8. Thou shalt not steal thy colleague's constituency if thine is rendered less winnable by boundary changes.

9. Thou shalt not bear false witness unless it is in the House of Commons where you can claim parliamentary privilege.

10. Thou shalt not covet thy neighbour's appearance on *Newsnight* – yea, even unto his being interviewed by Jeremy Paxman.

Anti-Semitic Mel Gibson and his Holocaust-denying father, Hutton. *In vino veritas*, Mel.

Carbon offsetting. 'Going on a flight, are you? Give us some more money and we'll offset it for you.' Nice work if you can get it.

Prince Philip. He likes plain speaking, it's said. Except when it's directed at him. The freeloading xenophobic waste of space.

Our inner cities being no-go areas after dark.

Shaun Woodward. The turncoat's turncoat.

The fact that Britain has Europe's highest abortion rate and also Europe's highest rate of births to teenage mothers. You'd have thought the two facts would be mutually exclusive.

Oil and petrol companies boasting about their green credentials. The eco-fascists will hate you whatever you do or say so stop trying to appeal to them.

Paying farmers money *not* to grow things. Yeah, I know that, compared to the French, we're amateurs, but even so, it's wrong.

Mobile phone charges for international calls. They're taking the piss.

People who holiday in countries that aren't democracies – like Cuba. In principle, you shouldn't go to any country that doesn't allow its own citizens to leave.

People who holiday in countries that aren't democracies – and then boast about how 'cheap' everything is. And that's because…?

Spectators at golf tournaments who shout 'Get in the hole!' – especially after a tee shot.

Booker prize-winning novels. Especially when you think of great books that should have won the Booker Prize but weren't even nominated – e.g. *Birdsong, Captain Corelli's Mandolin, The Curious Incident of The Dog In The Night-Time, Monsignor Quixote.*

NHS A&E departments. We surrender our consumer rights and enter the Third World. The lack of resources, the grime and the resigned helplessness – you don't have to leave Britain to have a pretty good idea of what it must be like in sub-Saharan Africa. I once went to Charing Cross with my wife who had cut her leg in a road accident. While we were waiting – for

several hours – I noticed there was a man nursing a
pretty nasty head wound. So I went up to reception
and asked if he could be prioritized, only to be told
that they had a triage system, thank you very much,
and they didn't need my help to run it. At that
moment I spotted a group of nurses standing around
chatting. This wasn't a much-needed momentary
respite, they were having a good old chinwag. So I
pointed out the man with the head injury, only to be
told there was nothing they could do until a doctor
had seen him. 'I understand,' I said, not under-
standing, 'but couldn't you just give him a little tea
and sympathy in the meantime?' They looked at me as
if I had just trodden in something extremely unpleasant,
which, judging by the state of the hospital, I probably
had, and carried on chatting. OK, so my experience is
anecdotal but then what else do I have to go on?
Except for one thing: the government's target for A&E
is that 90 per cent of people should be seen within
four hours. What a typically unambitious target. What
a typically high safety net. So, basically, you are fine so
long as you are not one of the 10 per cent who finds
themselves spending the night on a trolley. Even then
you stand a good chance of being sat next to a drunk
who will offer you a sip of his Special Brew to make
up for the fact that he has just vomited over you. Of
course, if you are a government minister, your experiences will be completely different. If there is one thing
I hate about government ministers, even more than all
the other things I hate about them, it is the way they
boast about using the NHS. And why wouldn't they
use it? Not for them and their family the endless waits

and the inexcusable indignities. The triage system hasn't been invented that would send one of their children to the back of the queue. For the rest of us there is the ghastly democracy of the lowest common denominator.

Unemployed doctors in a country where there's a chronic shortage of doctors. (See NHS A&E departments.)

Politicians demanding state funding for political parties. They say that politics needs political parties: political parties can only run with money – hence state funding. But state funding is public funding: in other words, it's our money raised in taxes. This leads on to a much bigger question: why do we pay tax? It's really not that hard. We do so because we want clean, bug-free hospitals that treat people promptly, schools that produce well-educated students who shouldn't have to pay top-up fees when they go to university, and first-rate emergency services as a matter of right not luck. We want our borders to be rigorously defended – not only from armed aggressors but also from the threat of illegal immigrants: we do not expect to discover that eight out of ten refugees who are refused asylum remain in the UK. If we or our fellow citizens lose our jobs, we want social security while we look for new ones, and we want our elderly, who've paid into the system all their working lives, to be treated with the dignity they deserve. That's about the size of it. There's more than enough money washing around the system to provide for all of that but if there have to be cuts, then there are other things that we're prepared to

sacrifice, like all the unnecessary public-sector jobs devoted to sexual and gender awareness, social engineering and lifestyle coaching. Not to mention the funding of political parties.

Police prosecuting motorists where a warning would suffice. Just because the police can only do their job with the consent of the public doesn't mean that they should always pick on the people who consent to be policed. So thanks for those three points for doing 63mph on a 50mph road that used to have a speed limit of 70mph, you merciless, humourless, ignorant pair of bastards.

The loathsome BNP's attempts to portray itself as representative of the people when it is, in fact, a collection of evil racists.

Charities that send unsolicited Christmas cards and expect you to pay for them or send them back.

Government ministers in limousines instructing their chauffeurs to go through bus lanes to beat the traffic.

Squeegee merchants washing my car at the traffic lights – when I've specifically asked them not to.

Parents who ban their children from watching *any* TV.

Having to queue for hours in A&E while drunks – who are (or so you'd have thought) anaesthetized against their injuries – are given priority because the hospital wants to get rid of them.

The government's neglect of the countryside and its evident contempt for the people who live there.

Computer viruses and the idiots who write and spread them.

Sir Mark Thatcher. As horrible as his twin sister is delightful. Creep punched me when we were at prep school. He was thirteen and I was nine. Enough said.

Segregationists. Ancient and modern.

Being lectured to by Bob Geldof. It's wrong even when he's right.

The use of the word 'partner' instead of 'spouse'. Time was when the automatic assumption was that two parents were married. Now the automatic assumption is that they aren't. Don't believe me? Then go to a fathers' paternity class at any urban maternity hospital and you'll see what I mean.

Our post-shame society. Now the only crime that confers shame – genuine shame – on the criminal is anything involving the abuse of children. Well, that's fair enough but what about crimes of violence, thefts and other bad acts that impact on the rest of us? Shouldn't the perpetrators of those also feel – or be made to feel – bad for what they've done?

TV commercials that don't just subvert the truth but totally invert it. In the real world, the mum who loves her family shows this by cooking them a meal made from fresh

FURY

ingredients; in the world of TV ads, she serves them convenience food that, in the case of the cook-chill lasagne served
without vegetables, looks like a plate of cat sick.

Flowers by the side of the road after car crashes. I
blame Princess Diana. Well, at any rate, her death.
Grief used to be a private affair but then Di died and
the nation just let it all hang out. It wasn't enough to
be sad: you had to say it with flowers. The best that
can be said for those lachrymose weeks in September
1997 is that it was a good time to be a florist. You can
see the legacy of this emotional incontinence on roads
up and down the country. I understand people's shock
and sorrow when someone they know dies in a road
traffic accident but is that any reason to tie bouquets
round lamp-posts? Wouldn't they be better off giving
flowers to bereaved relatives or even making a
donation to an appropriate charity in the name of the
deceased? Surely either of those would be preferable to
commemorating the site or cause of death. I mean,
when my stepmother died of lung cancer I didn't put a
posy in her tobacconist's.

The effective decriminalization of so-called 'soft' drugs.

Losing work on a computer. Always
infuriating. Never ameliorated by
friends saying, 'You should have backed
it up.' Or, worse, telling you about T.E.
Lawrence who was obliged to rewrite *Seven
Pillars of Wisdom* after losing the only
manuscript while changing trains at

Reading station in 1919. The difference between me and Lawrence – besides the talent, the heroism and everything else – is that he was a masochist and so probably enjoyed bad things happening to him.

Drunk men having to take responsibility for what they do on a date when drunk women don't have to.

Paedo-hysteria that sees parents being told they can't take photos of their children playing football or appearing in school plays for fear that the photographs might fall into the hands of paedophiles. The way the paedo-hysterics tell it, there's a paedophile on every corner and no child is safe. In delivering that message, these doom-mongers are consoling paedophiles by assuring them that there are many people like them and poisoning the well of goodwill that exists between adults and children. Indeed, the paedo-hysteria has reached such a crescendo that it's impossible for an adult to say hello to an unaccompanied child or, worse, for a child in trouble to seek help from a stranger. In fact, the paedo-hysteria is even more corrosive than that. If men are put through increasingly tighter hoops before they're allowed to become, say, scoutmasters, then what sort of man – apart from a determined paedophile – is going to want to bother?

The removal of the hereditary peers from the House of Lords – only to be replaced by Labour cronies to scrutinize and amend the bills that Labour lobby fodder send up from the Lower House. Meet the new Lords, worse than the old Lords. And yes, we've all been fooled again.

The state's assessment of parental income when it comes to grants for further education. People go to university at the age of eighteen, which makes them adults. Why should their parents' income have the slightest relevance to their tuition fees? It doesn't in any other area of public finance. I'm not means-tested if my mother needs a new hip; my sister's income isn't taken into account if her brother-in-law needs a council house: why should something as vital as education be subjected to such stringency?

The government's attempts to introduce road pricing. Those of us who don't sit in the back of ministerial limos already pay for the privilege of driving our cars through the road fund licence and fuel tax at the rate of 80 per cent. We really don't need yet another tax on our cars.

Making geese livers explode to make pâté de foie gras. Where are the animal rights activists when you want them?

Successful people whose children are screwed up. It nullifies all their success.

The licence fee. The BBC's always telling us – in those gaps between programmes where the commercials should be – what great value the licence fee is but nothing is good value when you're obliged to buy it regardless of whether you want to use it or not. It's a matter of human rights. In a modern democracy, access to television is a right not a luxury and to make people pay for the medium itself is as absurd as charging them

for the right to read newsprint before they can buy the newspaper of their choice. How is a single pensioner (under the age of 75) supposed to be able to afford one and a half week's pension? Where do unemployed people, subsisting on benefits, find such a relatively huge sum? Why should students, already laden with debts, have to pay for channels they'll rarely – if ever – watch? What I don't get is why the licence fee is championed by the very same people who were against the poll tax on the basis that it didn't differentiate between the rich and the poor. Yet what is the licence fee if it isn't a poll tax? When you point this out, they invariably reply, 'Of course, no one needs to have a television.' This is nonsense: in a modern democracy, access to such an important source of information is as vital – if not more so – as the right to vote itself. Don't get me wrong, I do recognize the need for public-service broadcasting. There is an excellent case for having a single BBC TV channel and a couple of national radio stations dedicated to the sort of programming – news, documentaries, the arts – that the market can't or won't provide. It would cost a fraction of the BBC's current budget and it could be funded by a mixture of government grant, subscription, sponsorship and private donation. But the licence fee, in its present form, is simply wrong. Hellishly wrong.

Che Guevara T-shirts and posters. The guy was either a heartless murdering communist or a CIA stooge. Or, indeed, both. That does NOT make him a poster boy.

The absence of bobbies on the beat. I know it's almost become a cliché but that's because it is a very real problem. There has to be a connection with the rise in street crimes as they're not even there to provide a visible deterrent. There used to be a randomness to police presence. You never knew when you might bump into a copper – and nor did criminals. I know it's only anecdotal but let me tell you about where I live in Sussex. My nearest police station is in Arundel. It's closed in the evenings. If I know that, then burglars know that, too. They can go about their 'work' in the knowledge that the only people who can stop them are householders and we've been warned – in no uncertain terms – what will happen if we take the law into our own hands. A while back, I was in Worthing when I saw a gang of youths vandalizing a public phone-box. As luck would have it, I was next door to the police station. So I popped in ... only to find that it was shut. The phone that was supposed to put me through to a switchboard somewhere was broken (ironically enough). Later, I spotted two policemen talking to a motorist in a layby – presumably they were booking him for speeding. It may not be empirical evidence but it'll do as a snapshot of contemporary policing. By and large, a country gets the police force it deserves. Our police are no less effective – and certainly a lot more honest – than any other country's. The trouble is that apart from when it comes to major crimes like murder and rape, they don't share the priorities of the people they are supposed to serve. While we care about our children, our homes and our safety on the streets, the police are obsessed with

motorists and speeding. You can see why. A motorist represents a safe way of feeling a collar. They discover a crime and solve it in the time it takes to put on a siren. When I talk about 'the police', I should explain that the responsibility for police priorities lies not with decent coppers who entered the service with the best of intentions but with their bosses, the Chief Constables, who have a politically correct agenda that is sensitive to every -ism going, except 'criticism' from the very people who pay their salaries. We don't ask for much. We want protection in our homes; we want protection in our towns and cities. Above all, we want fewer police in cars and more on foot.

People who share their colds with us. The worst are the ones who slobber all over you as soon as you see them and then tell you about how awful they're feeling. Hey, no need to tell us, pal: we'll know in three days' time.

Envy. It's the ulcer of the soul. (See Meanness.)

Stage psychics. Complete cons. All of them.

Lies about global warming.

Politicians taxing us on the basis of those lies.

People driving too slow in front of us when we're in a hurry.

Cold calls from telephone canvassers – even though I'm ex-directory.

How You Should Deal With *Unwanted* Callers:

Ask them if they're real or just one of the voices in your head.

Ask them to spell their name. Then ask them to spell the name of their company. Then ask them where the company is located. Then ask them to spell the company's location.

Tell them to talk very VERY S-L-O-W-L-Y, because you want to write down every single word.

If they're phoning from a kitchen company, tell them you live in a squat.

If they say they're not selling anything, tell them that that's a pity because you're in the mood for buying.

If they give you their name – 'Hi, I'm Sharon' – say, 'Oh, Sharon, how ARE you?' as though they are a long-lost friend.

Tell them you're busy at the moment and could you have their home phone number to call them back later.

Persistent shoplifters not being treated as the criminals they truly are.

Pompous snobbish socialists. And let's not forget our hatred for socialists who buy lots of houses. Or indeed socialists who love humanity but hate people.

GOVERNMENT CITIZENSHIP TESTS

HERE'S A SAMPLE.

1. Is English ... ?

a) My first language.
b) My second language.
c) Yes, some sort of language, I think.

2. Why have you applied for British citizenship?

a) Because I think I've got a real contribution to make to this country.
b) I'm sorry, I thought this was the form for housing benefit.
c) So that I won't get deported if I break the law.

3. Do you have any communicable diseases, such as TB?

a) No, but you're welcome to test me.
b) I have no idea.
c) I know my rights.

4. Do you know the words of the National Anthem?

a) Yes – all of them, including the verses that you lot don't know.
b) I think I could probably hum it.
c) No, and I have no intention of ever learning it.

5. What are speed cameras?

a) An unnecessarily harsh and intrusive means of gathering revenue.

b) Things that flash at me while I'm cleaning windscreens at traffic lights.

c) A vital tool in road safety.

6. What are euros?

a) Mickey Mouse money that we Brits should have nothing to do with.

b) Ah, you mean the money I gave to that lorry driver in Calais?

c) The currency of a united Europe that we must join as soon as possible.

7. What is toad-in-the-hole?

a) A dish of sausages in batter.

b) Yes, hang on, I am seeing the *Carry On* ... film only yesterday.

c) Yet another example of cruelty in the British countryside.

8. How good is your history? Why is Waterloo so important?

a) It's where Britain defeated France in 1815.

b) It was the song with which Abba won the Eurovision Song Contest.

c) It was the station I arrived at clinging to the underside of the Eurostar.

9. Now for a question on the law. You are a burglar. One day, while going about your work, you slip on a house-holder's roof. Do you ... ?

a) Only have myself to blame.

b) Go along to Accident & Emergency where I will of course have a 90 per cent guarantee of being treated within four hours.

c) Phone my immigration lawyer and ask him if he handles compensation cases.

10. Who is David Cameron?

a) The leader of the Conservative Party.

b) A future contestant on *I'm A Celebrity. . . Get Me Out Of Here!*

c) Nope, I've no idea.

11. What happened on 30 July 1966?

a) England won the World Cup.

b) Search me – I was up all night revising questions on *EastEnders.*

c) Harriet Harman turned sixteen.

12. What will you do if your application to become a citizen is rejected?

a) Abide by the decision.

b) Stay in the country as an illegal immigrant.

c) Get myself a lawyer from Matrix Chambers to handle my appeal.

13. If you become a citizen, what will be your opinion on asylum seekers?

a) I'm sorry but this is a small country and it's full.
b) I think they should be judged on a case-by-case basis.
c) Let 'em all in.

HOW YOU SCORED

Mostly As: We can do without your sort over here — go back to where you came from.

Mostly Bs: Nearly there but you're going to have to spend a few weeks at a converted holiday camp before you retake your test.

Mostly Cs: Congratulations! You are now a British citizen. Here's a house, a washing machine and your first month's benefits.

Wealthy people who announce that they're not leaving their money to their children but to charity. There's room in hell for all of you.

Global warming. The people who are banging on about global warming today are the same people who were warning us about a new ice age twenty years ago. In fact, the wise money is still on cold rather than warm but eco-fascists aren't going to spread that message because there is nothing we can do about an encroaching ice age and so there is no mileage – and therefore no massive grants – in it for them. Basically, global warming is just an opportunity for former communists/anti-capitalists to beat up the West. Besides, it's no good us in the concerned West washing out Marmite jars if the rest of the world keeps pumping crap into the atmosphere. There's no point in us acting locally if the rest of world won't even *think* globally. But that is to expect logic in what has become a matter of faith. In the Godless West, environmentalism is not a cause: it is an infallible religion. I'm sorry but I don't care about a bunch of Brazilians who don't even play football. I'm sorry but I don't give a damn about endan-gered species of insects that I would swat if they came into my living room. I'm sorry but I will offer physical harm to the very next smug git who tells me: 'We didn't inherit the earth from our parents, we borrow it from our children.' Have you noticed that environmentalism always means having to say you're sorry? Yeah, well, I'm sorry but the truth is I'm not sorry.

Community 'elders' getting all chippy at the prospect of a 'backlash' against that community in the wake of a terrorist atrocity or a spate of knifings. If you're going to open your mouths then do so to apologize to the rest of us and to demand that *your* community cleans up its act. Otherwise, you're not part of the solution – just part of the problem.

The inevitability of hosepipe bans – no matter how many floods we have.

Local authorities threatening to close grammar schools. Whatever else is wrong with education, it isn't the few remaining grammar schools, but some councils are still doing their damnedest to abolish them. What motivates people to destroy proven centres of excellence? Is it ignorance, jealousy or simply a warped sense of 'equality' that invariably leads to a levelling down? Sometimes I think I'd like to get inside the minds of such people – but only after kicking their heads in first.

President Mahmoud Ahmadinejad of Iran. Crazy name, crazy guy.

People who criticize Israel for taking President Mahmoud Ahmadinejad of Iran seriously when he says that a) the Holocaust never happened and b) he's going to nuke Israel.

Princess Michael of Kent. Turns even the most ardent monarchist into a republican.

 FURY

Stamp duty. So wrong for so many reasons. Why should we have to pay a tax – out of taxed income – just to buy a home?

Obvious miscarriages of justice. Like poor sods who are sent down for high-profile murders when all they're guilty of is being a bit odd. All right, very odd.

'YOU ALREADY **KNOW**
ENOUGH TO GO
TO **HELL**.'

David A. Christensen

e environment with our cars before
rders private planes to jet off to destin
ons served perfectly well by schedul
ights. People who go bankrupt but st
njoy a high standard of living. It's ev
orse when they fail to pay the 'litt
ictims – like the newsagents. Di
ospitals harbouring antibiotic-resista
ugs. What I don't get is that traffic pol
predicated on the basis that even if
ves just one li... it's worth putting
peed hump/c... the speed lim
nstalling s... as to why do
ealth chiefs... clean wards a
oilets – w... would arrest t
pread of M... very minimu
equirement? ...ch... er. There a
o word. The only silver lining to t
oud he... ought of wh
itchen staff... the world could
o his f... died peop
ho w... edie... for th
ars. Private... bastar
e lot of the... savage do
ho are asto... when their do
avage their... e was always
entle – neve... ed a soul.' Un
amson decide... chew Kylie's face rig
ff. These a... ourse the same d
wners who, before... arrival, wou
oast, 'Samson's a great big s... Mi
ou, if someone so much as looks at
he wrong way, 'e'd tear their facki
eart aht.' The left's blind eye to hum
ghts' violations in Africa and the Mid
ast when it's Africans oppress

# RAGING FURY

Anti-Americans whose anti-Americanism is so virulent that they end up supporting Islamic terrorists.

Fortnightly rubbish collections. Invariably coupled with increased council tax.

Innocent citizens getting arrested for standing up to yobs. If you're a shopkeeper and a 'youth' steals from you, why shouldn't you run after him? And why shouldn't you restrain him to stop him running off before the police arrive? And how *dare* they arrest *you* for trying to safeguard your livelihood?

President-for-life Fidel Castro. Clue's in the name. How come the same lefty comics who hate Bush have such a hard-on for a man who's never submitted himself to a genuine election since he seized power nearly fifty years ago? And if these self-same bastards hate Guantanamo Bay so much, why don't they say something about all the political prisoners in Castro's prisons? Obviously, I'm looking forward to the day

when the tyrant dies, but it will be spoiled by all those tossers eulogizing him.

Yobs regarding their ASBOs with pride.

The shabby treatment of elderly folk in many NHS hospitals. If they're not stuck on trolleys or sent home hours before a much-needed operation, they're often not fed or bathed properly and suffer from bedsores. I'm haunted by the story of an old woman who was desperate for an ice cream one night but couldn't find a nurse with the patience to help her. She died the following morning. Even prisoners on Death Row get a final meal (often, ironically, including ice cream), but it was more than our so-called health service could manage.

Our under-equipped troops remaining in Iraq. We won the war relatively easily. We should have brought our troops home immediately after. MBEs all round. Why keep them there to play piggies in the middle while Sunnis and Shias conduct a civil war?

The cross-party veneration of the NHS when it's absolutely clear that it isn't 'fit for purpose' The NHS is the third biggest employer in the world (after the Russian Army and the Indian Railways) so is it any wonder that it's impossible to manage effectively? The good things that happen in NHS hospitals happen in spite of the system and/or because of decent doctors and nurses. No system should have to rely on outstanding individuals to make it function since no system is going to have that many outstanding individuals in its ranks. It should be abolished if that's the only way to deliver proper health care to the nation. Trouble is, no political party's got the bottle to do it. Even though it would result in better healthcare for *everyone.* The bottom line is that cancer survival rates are *twice* as good in the US as they are here. And that statistic is based on *all* Americans – the ones with insurance and the ones who rely on Medicare. We also have the worst cancer survival rates in the *whole* of western Europe. There was a time when the Conservative Party looked like it was going to do something substantial to improve the NHS to the point where, if necessary, it would be substantially dismantled and reconstituted to provide what this country needs – what this country is literally *dying* for: a dynamic system of healthcare that serves the needs of the people and not the system. The trouble is, under David 'Dave' Cameron, the party's sole interest seems to be to obtain power for its own sake and not to effect necessary change. Which leads us to the $64 billion question: is the NHS safe in Tory hands? God, I hope not, but I fear that it is.

Religious fundamentalists. Mad, bad and dangerous to know. The most scary ones – apart from the homicide bombers – are the ones who believe that people from all other faiths will go to Hell. In other words, it's not enough that they should be saved, others must be damned. Well, damn them too.

The United Nations. It's a joke organization that once boasted Syria on its Security Council, had Libya – yes, Libya – chairing its Human Rights Panel and currently has Zimbabwe heading up Sustainable Development. That's the same Zimbabwe (qv) that has politically induced famines and an inflation rate in excess of 3,000 per cent p.a. There should be minimum entry requirements – most importantly, evidence of functioning democratic institutions – and a minimum commitment of funds and resources. From that starting point, the UN would then have the right – and indeed the obligation – to go into any country guilty of such bad governance that the people are oppressed and/or starving.

Fellow-travellers and useful idiots who still refuse to acknowledge the evils of communism.

The Family Courts' routine discrimination against fathers. Specifically, fathers who are denied access to their children after divorce or following the break-up of a relationship, on the whim of the women from whom they have parted – often acrimoniously. The way that a generation of fathers has been forcibly estranged from their children is scandalous. They are the last persecutable minority, expected to take full part in their children's upbringing – until and unless the relationship ends and then the woman calls the shots. The rights of fathers are as important for men as universal suffrage was for women.

THE WORST NOISES IN THE WORLD

The noise of fingernails scratching a blackboard.

The noise of city-centre drunks at midnight on a Saturday.

The noise of the mechanic who sucks in his breath when he looks at your car.

The noise of someone taking their first violin lesson.

The noise of the police siren before you're pulled over.

The noise of a couple having a row in the next-door hotel room.

The noise of an ultra-sensitive car alarm.

The noise of a fly trapped in the bedroom when you're trying to sleep.

The noise of someone else's poorly tuned radio.

The noise of yobs larking around while you're all on the same train for the next three hours.

The American and British governments doing nothing about Zimbabwe. The country used to be the breadbasket of Africa but since Robert Mugabe gave 'war veterans' permission to seize white-owned farms the rural economy has collapsed. Even so, there would still be enough food to go around if it weren't for Mugabe's policy of withholding it from parts of the country where opposition supporters live. In other words, as in Russia (in the thirties), China (fifties) and Biafra (seventies), there's been a deliberate attempt to induce famine. But then that's how famines usually start. You probably know the old saying that no two democracies ever fought a war, but did you know that no democracy with a flourishing press has ever suffered a famine? We don't only have the right to do something about Mugabe and his murderous henchmen, we have a responsibility.

Prince Charles ticking us off for polluting the environment with our cars before he orders private planes to jet off to destinations served perfectly well by scheduled flights.

People who go bankrupt but still enjoy a high standard of living. It's even worse when they fail to pay the 'little' victims – like the newsagents.

Dirty hospitals harbouring antibiotic-resistant bugs. What I don't get is that traffic policy is predicated on the basis that even if it saves just one life, it's worth putting in speed humps/cutting the speed limit/installing speed cameras. So why don't health chiefs make ultra-clean wards and toilets – which alone would arrest the spread of MRSA – the very minimum requirement?

Michael Winner. There are no words. The only silver lining to the cloud he casts is the thought of what kitchen staff all over the world could do to his food. Please.

Able-bodied people who wangle disabled badges for their cars.

Private car-clampers. Utter bastards the lot of them.

Owners of savage dogs who are astonished when their dogs savage their baby. ''e was always so gentle – never 'armed a soul.' Until Samson decided to chew Kylie's face right off. These are, of course, the same dog owners who, before Kylie's arrival, would boast, 'Samson's a great big softy. Mind you, if someone so much as *looks* at me the wrong way, 'e'd tear their facking 'eart aht.'

The left's blind eye to human rights' violations in Africa and the Middle East when it's Africans oppressing Africans or Arabs oppressing Arabs. The way the left – and its mouth-piece, the BBC – cares so little for the rights of ordinary African and Arab people to enjoy the same democratic freedoms that we (and they) take for granted is just appalling. Black-on-black oppression and racism is as bad as white-on-black oppression and racism. To believe otherwise is itself racist.

Junkies and their habits. There are now 500 times more heroin addicts than there were in the sixties, two-thirds of drugs treatments don't work and nine out of ten addicts relapse. The number of 'problem' users doubles every four years. Only the mad or criminally irresponsible could deny that heroin and crack cocaine are the scourge of our age. These drugs kill thousands, destroy families and account for a large proportion of crime as addicts steal to feed their habits. Up to now, the policy of the state has been to target the dealers. This is understandable: they are, after all, the real villains. The users, on the other hand, are regarded as victims. They are not punished – certainly not for first offences – but are sent for treatment. When this fails (which it usually does), they are registered as users and given the heroin 'substitute' methadone, which is about as effective as telling a would-be suicide to jump from the thirty-third floor rather than the forty-fourth. The fact is the war against the supply of drugs is being lost. Nevertheless, we have to continue the fight, redoubling our efforts, while simultaneously opening up a new front: against the demand. Here's a suggestion. Let the Home Secretary announce that, precisely one year from now, heroin or crack cocaine possession would lead to a mandatory jail sentence. The reason for delaying this policy for a year would be to allow current users the opportunity to kick their addiction. To this end, the government would also provide effective rehabilitation. However, in twelve months' time, all bets would be off and offenders would be sent straight to new, drug-free prisons. If it sounds tough, it has to be, but we can pity addicts without indulging them. The point is that it

would marginalize the real addicts – the lost souls – from the occasional users, help to deter the next generation of adolescents from experimenting and would also help put the dealers out of business. Such a policy would be massively expensive, but the question is not can we afford to do it but can we afford not to?

Saudi Arabia's contempt for democracy.

Saudi Arabia's sponsorship of world terrorism.

Saudi Arabia's treatment of people they perceive to be criminals.

British people who go to work in Saudi Arabia.

British people who go to work in Saudi Arabia and pay no tax on their wages.

British people who go to work in Saudi Arabia and pay no tax on their wages who are then arrested for drinking.

British people who go to work in Saudi Arabia and pay no tax on their wages who are then arrested for drinking and are sentenced to a public beating.

British people who go to work in Saudi Arabia and pay no tax on their wages who are then arrested for drinking and are sentenced to a public beating and then whinge like girls and expect the British Foreign Office – which runs on the taxes that they DON'T pay – to intercede on their behalf.

Unlimited immigration. Why can't we apply the same tough criteria they use in less populous countries such as Canada, New Zealand and Australia? As for asylum seekers, let's take our fair share, so long as they come here as friends, not enemies. At the moment, Britain has a problem with Islamic fundamentalists. We don't need any more, thank you very much. However, by the same token, we should be happy to give refuge to victims of such fundamentalism. An Afghan, say, who has fled his country because of the Taliban should be welcomed, not resented.

Multi-millionaire pop stars telling us to make poverty history. Yes, you, Bono, you pious tax-avoiding boring tosser.

Anti-Semitism. The oldest hatred. The fact is there are so few Jews left that if the world were represented by a single man, the only part of him that would be Jewish is the fingernail of the smallest finger of one hand. Yet still anti-Semitism spreads throughout Europe like a disease from which there is no inoculation. Even in Britain, a country that has always had a proud record of tolerance, there are disturbing signs of anti-Semitism becoming 'fashionable'. Time was when all that British Jews had to fear was the pond life of the extreme Right; now it's the fascist Left who use Israel as a pretext to attack Jews. Why, if they care so much about the world's oppressed, don't they protest about Zimbabwe, Uganda, North Korea or Sudan? The truth is that the Fascist Left cares nothing about the oppressed: it is motivated not by compassion but by a visceral hatred for Jews and Judaism. Some of this hatred is predicated on anti-Americanism but a lot of it is just anti-Semitism, plain and evil.

Uninsured/unlicensed drivers. They should be banned for life. The right course of action is to target uninsured rather than unlicensed drivers, because you can have a licence without being insured but you can't be insured without a licence. Motorists should have to put proof of insurance on windscreens, but I have an additional suggestion: as the one constraint that no driver can avoid is the need to fill up with petrol or diesel, it should be made compulsory for drivers to produce a proof-of-insurance card – provided by their insurance companies – whenever they pay for fuel. It would be a bore but who can say it wouldn't be worth it?

Intensive farming that results in hens having their beaks cut, sows shut in steel stalls and other animals kept in appalling conditions. Obviously there has to be a balance between the needs of animals and the commercial interests of farmers. No one's calling for pigs to have masseuses and access to Jacuzzis but there is a happy medium and it's called free-range farming where creatures can roam freely without being force-fed antibiotics in an industrial process that disgraces us almost as much as it torments them.

Children who physically attack teachers. Such pupils are not dispossessed or disadvantaged: they are simply scum. Unfortunately, they're second-generation scum so they have no role models to look up to. Their parents dress and act like petulant teenagers with no thought for anything but their own immediate self-gratification. Their idea of parenting is neglect or, at best, an attempt to befriend their children. Children don't need this from parents: what they need from

them is certainty; to know where the boundaries are and to know what sanctions will be applied if they cross those boundaries. There are no sanctions for such children and therefore no boundaries. At least their grandparents knew to treat teachers with due respect so that when they were summoned to the school because of their child's misbehaviour, they were properly contrite and accepted the school's punishment. Indeed, they probably added to it once they returned home. These days, too many parents have a different attitude. If they bother to turn up at the school at all they too offer violence to the teacher. This further undermines discipline until an atmosphere of total lawlessness pervades the school. Let's get one thing perfectly clear: bad behaviour has nothing to do with 'lack of resources', the perennial *cri de coeur* of the agitating classes, and everything to do with violence for the malevolent sake of itself. Children who attack teachers must be removed from mainstream education. Immediately.

Meanness. It's a disease of the soul.
(See Envy.)

Wishy-washy Church of England clerics who wring their hands in horror at things done by the government but remain strangely silent about the persecution of Christians in Muslim countries.

The NHS's managerial and clerical staff rising as the number of NHS beds falls.

People who poison the well. You'll note that I haven't listed murderers, rapists and armed robbers because I take it as read that we're all against such people. However, it is worth including them in the book – not for what they've done to their victims (which is obviously evil) but for how they poison the well for the rest of society. For example, when a man rapes a woman who has flagged down his car when hers has broken down on the motorway, he doesn't just destroy her life, he also stops women generally from trusting men. All because of the actions of one evil man. It's not fair.

Commuters crammed on to dirty, overcrowded trains. They're a captive market – and that's why, of course, they're treated so wretchedly. The fact is that it's entirely predictable how many people will be using rush-hour trains: the train companies could quite easily put on enough trains with sufficient carriages to provide seats for all their passengers. Especially as they can be sure that those very same trains and carriages will be needed for the return journey. Airline passengers are guaranteed seats: why should railway passengers be treated worse? These days, it costs a damn sight more to travel by train than it does to fly. It comes down to simple fairness. Commuters commute because they're going to work. They're the people who pay for the people who remain at home – the pensioners, the home-makers and the unemployed. They're net givers. They're entitled to be able to sit down before and after a day's work.

The Burmese government's persecution of the wonderful Aung San Suu Kyi.

The Catholic Church's collusion in child abuse. Perhaps the most obscene aspect of the Vatican's cover-up of the sexual abuse of children was the way it backed its imposition of secrecy with the warning of excommunication. If only the Catholic Church had threatened the guilty priests with the same penalty, just think how many children could have been spared.

NICE rationing cancer drugs on the basis of cost when the NHS wastes billions every year. Made even worse by the NHS demanding that any cancer sufferer who has the temerity to pay for a cancer drug that has been denied to them on the NHS then has to pay for *all* their treatment. In other words, unless you're extremely wealthy, you're condemned to second-class care.

George Galloway.

Western responses to African famines. The fact is, by propping up corrupt and inefficient governments, we in the West are colluding in keeping the people in starvation. Looking at starving children, it seems impossible not to conclude that the answer is more food, but that's like looking at a spate of vandalized windows and assuming that the answer's more glaziers. Perhaps it's time to do something about the vandals. Many African leaders are political and economic vandals. They loot and pillage their countries as a matter of course. Then they hold out their hands to the West. It's all very well for people to say, 'Cancel Third World debt', but have they ever stopped to consider why there's a debt in the first

place? It's because these wretched leaders have to borrow, and why do they borrow? Because they're inefficient and corrupt. It's the most vicious of vicious circles. Africa is full of fertile countries, rich in minerals; African people are keen to work; Africa should be a success. It isn't – because potentates are squandering their countries' GDPs on palaces and numbered Swiss bank accounts, and massive armies to protect those interests, while denying their people democratic human rights. The most basic of which is food in their bellies. The only political system that works is democracy; the only economic system that works is capitalism. The $15 billion – BILLION – that George Bush promised to combat Aids in the Third World didn't come out of a command economy like Ethiopia's, where the state owns all the land and the people starve, but from a capitalist democracy. Bush's Left-leaning, sanctimonious, self-righteous critics say $15 billion's not enough but then they would say that. You'll note, however, that they don't put their hands in their own pockets. Instead, they call for the drug companies to hand over free medicines. But why should they? Protecting their patents is how they make money. If they didn't make money there wouldn't be any research and development, which means there wouldn't be any new drugs. Anti-capitalist demon-strators might not like it but they'll be grateful when their own lives need saving. Why would they deny African people a system that would do the same for them? Unfortunately, we in the West don't like to say anything because it might be meddling with their 'culture'. But any culture – any system – that can't

feed its own people forfeits its right to immunity from interference. Why do we have so little confidence in Africans? Why do we have such low expectations for them? Is it because they 'is' black? Is that why the same people who were so hard on apartheid in South Africa are so reluctant to tackle Zimbabwe or any of the other African hellholes? Democracy's good enough for us, then why not for Africa? There are children simply dying for it.

Burglars being let off with a caution. It should be a month inside per burglary as a basis for negotiation – and no bloody TICs. Why don't the police take burglary as seriously as we, the public, do? For many victims, particularly women, burglary is a violation – nothing less – which can lead to life-altering conditions like anxiety/depression and worse. At the very least, we must end the ludicrous restrictions on householders' attempts at self-protection. Why shouldn't burglars be put on notice that, as in the US, their 'rights' end the moment they enter our homes? Such a policy wouldn't, as liberals claim, give householders the right to torture and/or murder intruders but it would give us the right to use reasonable force to defend ourselves, our families and our homes. And it would also mitigate any 'unreasonable' force used in the heat of the moment. The combination of automatic jail sentences and possible retribution by householders would go a long way to deterring what is – or should be – a truly serious crime.

University tuition fees. The hated Tories were in government for eighteen years – eleven under the control of the evil Thatcher – but it wasn't them who introduced university tuition fees. Nope, it was New Labour – within about a day of taking power. How typical of the party that abolished the grammar school to stop another generation of working-class kids from self-advancement. It's called pulling up the ladder after you yourself have got to the top and it's a deeply unpleasant thing to do.

Mark Oaten. What you did was SOOOOOOO disgusting, you should have retired entirely from public life.

Roads that have so many speed humps they're more like obstacle courses. In Hell, the roads aren't paved with good intentions but with speed humps. These wretched lumps of concrete that blight our roads and wreck our car exhausts are always justified on the basis that 'they save lives'. But that's not even true. According to the London Ambulance Service, speed humps are responsible for hundreds of deaths a year. Apparently, for every life saved through 'traffic calming', more are lost because of ambulance delays. That's it. End of argument. In a sane society, the verdict of the London Ambulance Service would be heeded and acted upon: speed humps would be ripped up and there would be a ban on any new ones. But this is a wicked, venal society and so these loathsome obstacles continue to proliferate. And why? Not because the powers-that-be care about pedestrians (on the contrary:

we now know they are more likely to die) but because they don't like motorists. Motorists are too independent; they must be brought to heel. This explains the obsession with speed cameras. Once again, the justification is 'they save lives' but that's also open to question. Motoring experts insist that cameras on dual carriageways and motorways cause more accidents than they prevent because drivers brake suddenly. Never mind, it's a handy source of revenue, even if it is derived from motorists who have bought taxed cars with tax discs out of taxed income and filled them with taxed petrol, and it shows us who's boss.

Rogue car alarms that go off then stop for a couple of minutes before resuming. Ad infinitum.

The 'mmm ... Danone' sting at the end of ads for Danone products.

Osama Bin Laden. Come on, mate, outside the cave – if you think you're hard enough.

Brian Sewell's voice. Look, he's not the only person in the world with an annoying voice – there are plenty of others, such as Nadia Sawalha, Jane Horrocks, Alan Davies, Ben Fogle, Michael Winner, Prince Charles, Jilly Goolden, Bill Oddie and Ruth Kelly – but, when it comes to getting on my nerves and tits and going straight up my nose, his transcends not only every

other voice in the world but also almost any other thing. That's why he's made it all the way to Chapter 7. If there is a Hell, then I reckon that every single announcement will be made by someone who sounds just like him. And that's how I'll know – for sure – that it really is **HELL**.

TARGETS I REFUSED TO GO FOR

The *Daily Mail*. I'm an Express man, but I have to acknowledge that this is a damn fine paper.

Coleen McLoughlin. She's not a bad lass.

Chavs. I don't go on turkey shoots. Well, not always.

Channel 4's programme schedules. Curate's egg.

Microsoft. Works for me.

Jimmy Carr. I know he does a lot of corporate work but he's still a good comic.

Motorway service stations. It's not that I like them especially but they're there to satisfy a need, not to be aesthetically pleasing.

McDonald's. I don't know that it uses up any more of the earth's natural resources – including the bloody rainforests – than any other restaurant on a per person per meal basis.

Sting. Yeah I know, but at least he's written some nice tunes.

Germaine Greer. Wrong on nearly everything but a game old bird.

James Blunt. Annoying but at least the guy's served his country.

Jeffrey Archer. Undoubtedly annoying but *First Among Equals* was a good read and he has served his time.

Muzak. It's quite nice if truth be told.

Natasha Kaplinsky. No worse than any other fame-hungry over-made-up female newsreader.

Piers Morgan. So what if he's got the hide of a walrus and more front than Sainsbury's? He adds to the gaiety of the nation.

Robbie Williams. So it's not art – but he does suffer for it.

George W. Bush. Not the smartest cookie in the barrel, eh? You don't say. But he was democratically elected – well, at least once – and he will be going soon. And when you think what damage he could have done... Also, I hate people who are anti-Bush more than I hate the man himself.

Airline food. I like it.

Music festival toilets. Serves 'em right for eating too many lentils.

Garage flowers. They've saved my bacon on more than one occasion.

Wembley Stadium. They finished it eventually.

Ann Widdecombe. Mad as a box of frogs but quite sweet really.

Fruit machines in pubs. The best thing about the wretched places.

Chris Moyles. I'm sure he's as awful as his critics say he is but I've never listened to him.

Doctors' receptionists. Much better than they used to be.

John McCririck. Can't be as bad as he looks. Surely?

London cabbies. The best in the world. Or so they themselves say.

Richard & Judy. Not while there's a chance of getting into their Book Club.

Cream crackers. Yes, I know they split into three whenever you try to butter them. So use margarine instead.

Tesco. It's not their fault they've got such a huge share of the marketplace. I guess they just give people what they want. Perhaps other retailers should take note.

Coldplay. Not necessarily worse than any other modern band. But certainly more successful – hence the flak.

Spam emails for penis enlargement. You never know when it might come in useful…

Jamie Oliver. Irritating, I grant you, but he's not wrong, you know.

Traffic wardens. Look, no one – least of all me – wants to get parking tickets but if traffic wardens didn't exist, there wouldn't be anywhere to park in our city centres because other people would park their cars there all day long. Still, I grant you that it is annoying to see traffic wardens swarming on streets where no police officer is ever seen.

Sir Ben Kingsley. His apparent insistence that everyone addresses him by his title makes him sound a bit of a tartar. So here's a word in his defence. In 1985, three years after his Oscar-winning triumph in *Gandhi*, he was at a party where a woman prattled on endlessly about how absolutely brilliant he'd been in *The Jewel In The Crown*. Did he sulk, scream or even correct her? No, he waited for her to realize her mistake and then laughed like a good sport. I have been teasing my wife about it ever since.

Acknowledgements

This book (like all books) was a team effort – even though I took great care to ensure that mine was the only name on the cover. So it gives me great pleasure to acknowledge the invaluable help of (in alphabetical order) Luigi Bonomi, Rich Carr, Mari Roberts, Penny Symons and last – but very much not least – the peerless Doug Young.

In addition, I'd also like to thank the following people for their help, contributions and/or support: Gilly Adams, Alison Barrow (not least for supplying the title), Jeremy Beadle, Marcus Berkmann, Alison Bonomi, Paul Donnelley, Jonathan Fingerhut, Jenny Garrison, Richard Littlejohn, Kelvin Mackenzie, Vanessa Milton, William Mulcahy, Emma Musgrave, Bryn Musson, Amanda Preston, Molly Stirling, Charlie Symons, Jack Symons, Louise Symons, David Thomas and Rob Woolley.

Finally, every week I write a column for the *Sunday Express* which includes a section entitled 'We've Had Enough Of...' to which readers are invited to contribute. This book includes many of those contributions and so I would like to express my sincere gratitude to them and indeed to Rachel Jane, the editor of my column, and to Martin Townsend, the editor of the paper.